Ron Comfort
Titus 2:13

LAST THINGS

A Book on Bible Prophecy

Dr. Ron Comfort

To order more copies of *Last Things,* contact Dr. Ron Comfort:

Dr. Ron Comfort
Ambassador Baptist College
PO Box 158
Lattimore, NC 28089
704-434-0303
jcomfort@ambassadors.edu
www.ambassadors.edu

All Scripture quotations are from the King James Version of the Bible.

Last Things

Cover design: Mack Swaringen
Cover photo: http://www.istockphoto.com
Cover photo title: Planet in Danger
Design and page layout: Andrew Minion

Revised Printing, 2011.

ISBN 978-0-9712414-0-4

Table of Contents

In Appreciation

When I began work to put *Last Things* back in print, I soon realized that the first step was to gain the services of someone with the patience to take my messages from audio recordings to paper. An Ambassador Baptist College student's wife, Sandra Bickish, took on this daunting task. In addition to her duties as wife, she spent numerous hours transcribing the messages with great care. I am indebted to her for her hours of cheerful, careful labor in my behalf. Her first-step work got the project underway.

Since August 31, 1963, my wife Joyce has been my constant companion. We have undertaken many projects together, and without her assistance in refining the chapters of this manuscript, this book could not have been a reality. She has labored many hours editing, proofing, and preparing the manuscript for the publisher, and I am grateful.

The final product with its graphic flourishes and finishing touches is due to the talent, diligence, and care of Andrew Minion. Andrew is a graduate of Ambassador, and faithfully and cheerfully uses his talents and abilities for the Lord on the college staff and in his local church ministry. I am grateful to him for masterminding the layout of the book. His work has gone a long way in making *Last Things* attractive.

Finally, I am indebted to you, my readers. I pray that you will be challenged and changed for eternity through this study of last things.

Foreword

The first edition of *Last Things* was printed in 1977. After some revisions, the book was reprinted in 1985, and as I established Ambassador Baptist College in 1989, the last copies of that second edition had just been exhausted. For several years, I wanted to do a third printing, but commitments to the college and my ministry of itinerant evangelism precluded my doing so.

After being president of Ambassador Baptist College for twenty years, in 2009 I felt the time was right to put new leadership in place. God has abundantly blessed the college ministry in the transition to the leadership of Dr. Alton Beal.

Among the projects that I hope to complete before the Lord takes me Home is the reprint of several books that have been out of circulation for some time. It is my prayer that these efforts will be helpful to mature Christians and to point people to Christ.

For those who may have read the first printing of *Last Things*, you will notice many changes in this new edition. I endeavored to eliminate some messages and include others of greater importance. The book is, by and large, a study of eschatology and could easily be used as a manual for Sunday School lessons. The messages are clearly outlined so that a Sunday School teacher could use the outlines as a teaching tool.

I have avoided any sensationalism that often accompanies prophetic preaching. The basis for true prophetic preaching always ought be simply the Word of God.

People often ask me how long it takes to prepare particular prophetic messages. These messages have been prepared and refined over hundreds of hours. I have never tried to preach prophetically for the purpose of entertaining my listeners or readers. Rather, these messages are designed to be practical and to help Christians prepare their lives so that they will *"not be ashamed before Him at His coming."*

Chapter 1

The Rapture

In I Thessalonians 4:13–18, Paul writes,

> *But I would not have you to be ignorant, brethren, concerning them which are asleep, that ye sorrow not, even as others which have no hope.*
> *For if we believe that Jesus died and rose again, even so them also which sleep in Jesus will God bring with him.*
> *For this we say unto you by the word of the Lord, that we which are alive and remain unto the coming of the Lord shall not prevent them which are asleep.*
> *For the Lord himself shall descend from Heaven with a shout, with the voice of the archangel, and with the trump of God: and the dead in Christ shall rise first:*
> *Then we which are alive and remain shall be caught up together with them in the clouds, to meet the Lord in the air: and so shall we ever be with the Lord.*
> *Wherefore comfort one another with these words.*

These verses are the first really clear passage in the Bible on what is called the Rapture. Dr. H. A. Ironside made this statement: "One may go through Matthew, Mark, Luke, and John, and he will only find one Scripture that deals with the Rapture. That is John 14:3." I am not sure whether or not that is true, but I suspect that it is likely.

Some who have been Christians for a long time are still not aware that the Second Coming of Christ is in two phases. When He comes for those of us who are saved, His feet will not touch the earth; but we will be raised to meet Him in the air. That is the Rapture!

Some say, "Where do you find that word "rapture" in your English Bible?" It is not in our English Bible but is a transliteration, that is a foreign word that becomes a readily acceptable English word. The word "rapture" comes from the Latin word *rapto*. I Thessalonians 4:17: *"caught up together with them in the clouds"* is the phrase that best describes what happens at the *rapto* or Rapture.

After the Rapture of the church, there will be a seven-year period called the Tribulation when all the destruction of hell breaks loose on earth. The message you are now reading pertains to Act One of the drama, the Rapture. The Revelation of Christ follows the Tribulation and occurs when Christ comes back to Earth.

In my thorough study of the Scriptures regarding the return of Christ, I find only two Scriptures in the New Testament that mention both phases of the Second Coming in the same verse. For instance, I Timothy 4:1: *"I charge thee therefore before God, and the Lord Jesus Christ, who shall judge the quick and the dead at his appearing* (the Rapture) *and his kingdom* (the Revelation);" Again, Titus 2:13: *"Looking for that blessed hope* (the Rapture), *and the glorious appearing* (the Revelation) *of the great God and our Saviour Jesus Christ;"*

My primary focus in the study of our text passage in I Thessalonians is the Rapture. Notice several things concerning this exciting event.

The Rapture is a Sure Event.

I Thessalonians 4:16 states, *"For the Lord himself **shall** descend from Heaven with a shout..."* This event **shall** happen! I Corinthians 1:7–8: *"So that ye come behind in no gift; waiting for the **coming** of our Lord Jesus Christ:"* I Corinthians 4:5: *"Therefore judge nothing before the time, until the Lord **come**,"* Philippians 3:20: *"For our conversation*

is in Heaven; from whence also we look for the Saviour, the Lord Jesus
Christ:" Philippians 4:5: *"Let your moderation be known unto all men.*
The Lord is at hand." James said in James 5:8–9: *"Be ye also patient;*
stablish your hearts: for the coming of the Lord draweth nigh…behold,
the judge standeth before the door." Colossians 3:4: *"When Christ, who*
is our life, shall appear, then shall ye also appear with him in glory."
Hebrews 9:28: *"So Christ was once offered to bear the sins of many; and*
unto them that look for him shall he appear the second time without sin
unto salvation." What could be plainer than that? Jesus is coming a
second time!

In the one day that Jesus Christ died on Calvary's cross, there
were thirty-three Old Testament prophecies fulfilled. Imagine it—
thirty-three prophecies fulfilled in just one day! I was in Okinawa,
and after hearing that statement, the pastor asked one of his
military men who worked with computers to find out what the
chances are that thirty-three prophecies could be fulfilled in one
man in one day. The man returned with this startling percentage.
He said, "Pastor, the computer determined that the chances that
thirty-three prophecies could be fulfilled in one man in one day
are less than 1 in 87, with 92 zeroes after it." Think of that!

My friend, are you aware that in the life, the death, and the
resurrection of Christ, there were over three hundred Old
Testament prophecies fulfilled? Furthermore, for every one
promise in the Bible on the first coming of Jesus Christ you will
find twenty promises of the Second Coming of Jesus Christ. In
the New Testament there are 7,959 verses. Do you know that no
less than three hundred thirty verses in the New Testament alone
speak of the Second Coming of Jesus Christ? More is said about
King Jesus than is said about Baby Jesus. More is said in the Bible
about Jesus on the throne than even Jesus on a cross. Does it not
stand to reason that if all of the promises concerning Christ's first

coming were fulfilled, then surely all the promises concerning His Second Coming will also be fulfilled?

Every chapter in the books of I and II Thessalonians speaks of the Second Coming of Christ.

- I Thessalonians 1:10: *"And to wait for his Son from Heaven, whom he raised from the dead, even Jesus, which delivered us from the wrath to come."*

- I Thessalonians 2:19: *"For what is our hope, or joy, or crown of rejoicing? Are not even ye in the presence of our Lord Jesus Christ at his coming?"*

- I Thessalonians 3:13: *"To the end he may stablish your hearts unblameable in holiness before God, even our Father, at the coming of our Lord Jesus Christ with all his saints."*

- I Thessalonians 4:16: *"For the Lord himself shall descend from Heaven with a shout, with the voice of the archangel, and with the trump of God: and the dead in Christ shall rise first:"*

- I Thessalonians 5:23: *"And the very God of peace sanctify you wholly; and I pray God your whole spirit and soul and body be preserved blameless unto the coming of our Lord Jesus Christ."*

- II Thessalonians 1:7–8: *"And to you who are troubled rest with us, when the Lord Jesus shall be revealed from Heaven with his mighty angels, In flaming fire taking vengeance on them that know not God, and that obey not the gospel of our Lord Jesus Christ:"*

- II Thessalonians 2:1–2: *"Now we beseech you, brethren, by the coming of our Lord Jesus Christ, and by our gathering together unto him, That ye be not soon shaken in mind, or be troubled, neither by spirit, nor by word, nor by letter as from us, as that the day of Christ is at hand."*

- II Thessalonians 3:5: *"And the Lord direct your hearts into the love of God, and into the patient waiting for Christ."*

Any preacher that denies that Jesus Christ is coming again must tear the books of both First and Second Thessalonians from his Bible! Jesus is coming again. The Scripture verifies it!

I was preaching in Pittsburgh, and a lady came to me and said, "Brother Comfort, I went to my Presbyterian preacher and asked him if he believed in the Second Coming. He said that he didn't believe it, but that it really didn't matter if he believed it or not. What do you think about that?" How I wish that woman would have had sufficient backbone to say, "Pastor, I don't care whose seminary you went to or who may have told you that the Second Coming of Christ is unimportant, but it does matter because the Bible says it will happen!" She said, "Brother Comfort, I've been in that church ever since I've been a small girl. I can't leave that church now."

My heart is saddened for anyone who loves their denomination more than they love the Word of God. You may have gone to a church where in all of your life you have never one time heard a message preached on the Second Coming of Christ. You may say, "I don't know if my pastor believes it or not. I've never heard him say." My dear friend, if he has never said, then he does not believe it. If he does not believe in the Second Coming, then he likely does not believe in the verbal inspiration of the Word of God either. If he does not believe in the Second Coming, he probably does not believe in the virgin birth either. My friend, you need to leave that church, and go to a church where the Second Coming of Christ is believed and preached.

I was not reared in an independent Baptist home. For the first seven years of my life, I was a Roman Catholic. For the next eight years of my life, I was a Southern Baptist. When I was fifteen years of age, I was born again, and then I became an independent Baptist by conviction. However, I love the Bible far more than I love the tag "Independent Baptist." If the time ever comes when independent Baptists are known for their denial of the Second Coming, I will call myself by another name. I am not married to a denominational tag. God pity you if you love your denomination more than you love the Word of God. The Second Coming of Christ is a **sure event**.

The Rapture is a Sudden Event.

I Thessalonians 4:16: *"For the Lord himself shall descend from Heaven with a **shout**…:"* It is a sudden event. The word for "shout" in the Greek language means a military command. Jesus is coming with the shout of a military command. What will that command be?

You may recall that God's command to Noah was "Come in!" His command to Lot was "Come out!" His command to those of us who are saved is going to be "Come up!" Every child of God is going higher! Revelation 4:1: *"…and the first voice which I heard was as it were of a trumpet talking with me; which said, Come up hither, … ."* One day Jesus is coming in the air, and He will shout, "Come up hither!" I then will climb an invisible stairway to be with Jesus Christ. I Corinthians 15:51–52: *"Behold, I shew you a mystery; We shall not all sleep, but we shall all be changed, In a **moment**, in the twinkling of an eye, at the last trump: for the trumpet shall sound, and the dead shall be raised incorruptible, and we **shall be changed**."*

My dear friend, it is all going to happen in a moment, in the twinkling of an eye. Someone may say, "That is as quickly as you can blink your eye." No, my friend, it is quicker than that. An atom is the smallest unit of matter. May I say that the word twinkling is the same Greek word from which we get the word "atom." The Greek word for twinkling means the smallest unit of time. It is not the blinking of the eye; it is the sparkling of the eye—less than $\frac{1}{1000}$ of a second. Can you imagine that? In less than $\frac{1}{1000}$ of a second we are changed from a body of mortality into a body of immortality; from a body sown in weakness to a body raised in strength; from a body of corruption to a body of incorruption. Hallelujah!

Scientists tell us that the light from the farthest star has not yet reached the earth. They estimate that the light from the farthest star is five million light years away. What does that mean? Light travels at a speed of 186,000 miles per second. It would take 500 million years going at the rate of 186,000 miles per second for the light from the farthest star to ever reach the earth. Where is Heaven? Heaven is beyond the farthest star. Where is Jesus? Jesus is in Heaven. My dear friend, it is not going to take Jesus 500 million light years to come back to get His little children. He is coming in a moment, in the twinkling of the eye.

When Jesus was on earth, He told his disciples that He was coming again. He did not tell them when, but He intimated that He may come in their lifetime. For instance, in John 14:3, Jesus said, *"And if I go and prepare a place for **you**, I will come again, and receive **you** unto myself; that where I am, there **ye** may be also."* Luke 12:40: *"Be **ye** therefore ready also: for the Son of man cometh at an hour when ye think not."* Mark 13:35–36: *"Watch **ye** therefore: for ye know not when the master of the house cometh, at even, or at midnight, or at the cockcrowing, or in the morning: Lest coming suddenly he find **you** sleeping."*

I believe that every disciple in the New Testament was looking for Christ to come in his lifetime. The teaching of the New Testament never hints that you and I are to look forward to dying. We are not to look for the undertaker; we are to look for the Upper-taker. Peter was looking for the Lord. I Peter 5:4: *"And when the chief Shepherd shall appear, ye shall receive a crown of glory that fadeth not away."* John was looking for Christ. I John 2:28: *"And now, little children, abide in him; that, when he shall appear, we may have confidence, and not be ashamed before him at his coming."* Jude was looking for the return of Jesus. Jude 14: *"And Enoch also, the seventh from Adam, prophesied of these, saying, Behold, the Lord cometh with ten thousands of his saints,"* You and I are to live in constant expectation of the Second Coming of the Lord Jesus Christ.

I once spoke with an elderly lady in Indiana regarding the Second Coming of Christ. She said, "Brother Comfort, you are a young man." (Obviously this was not a recent conversation!) She said, "Now, you are a young man, and I am an old lady. Jesus may come in your lifetime, but I don't believe he's coming in my lifetime." Do you know what the Bible calls that? Three letters: S-I-N! I believe that the teaching of the Word of God is that we are to get up in the morning looking for the Second Coming of Jesus Christ. We are to go to bed at night thinking that perhaps before we ever awaken, Jesus may come to take us unto Himself.

D. L. Moody once said, "I never lay my head on my pillow at night but what I think the Son of Righteousness may dawn in the eastern sky and call me to be Home with Himself. I never begin my day's work but what I think this: Jesus may interrupt my work and begin His own work in me. My constant theme is 'perhaps today.'" That is the very way that you and I should live. The Second Coming of Jesus Christ is not put in the Bible to entertain us. It is put in the Bible to make a difference in how we live.

Looking for the Second Coming of Christ will produce two things in your life. First of all, it will produce the **inward look of preparation**. Almost every prophetic utterance in the Bible is accompanied by a practical application. Notice I John 3:2–3: *"Beloved, now are we the sons of God, and it doth not yet appear what we shall be: but we know that, when he shall appear, we shall be like him; for we shall see him as he is.* (That is a prophetic utterance.) *And every man that hath this hope in him **purifieth** himself, even as he is pure."* (That is the practical application.) No saved teenager who is looking for the Second Coming of Christ will feed on rock music. That is an impossibility! No adult who is truly looking for the Second Coming of Christ will live totally for pleasure and materialism.

On the closing night of a meeting I was preaching in Memphis, Tennessee, a lady brought a huge bag of rock music recordings to the pastor. She said, "Pastor, I am not a teenager, but I want this garbage out of my house." (Parent, if your children listen to rock music with your knowledge, you are not right with God.) The lady said, "Pastor I want you to break these things." Before breaking the records, the pastor turned over the record jacket on top and read the inscription. It said, "In the beginning, man created God; in the likeness of man, made he God." As he read that, there was a groan throughout the crowd. Sadly, one young man who was a student in the Christian school remarked to his friend, "I don't know why my preacher is breaking those rock records. I wish he would give them to me. I could put them to good use." In no way was that young man looking for the Second Coming of Jesus Christ.

My dear friend, if you are looking for the Second Coming of Jesus Christ, how can you allow R-rated videos to come into your house? How can you allow HBO or MTV to come into your living room if you are looking for the Second Coming of Christ? Anticipating the soon coming of Christ will prompt us to clean up our lives so that we will not be ashamed when He comes. If Jesus came right now, would you be ashamed to have Him see the things you have in your home?

Looking for the Second Coming of Christ will produce the inward look of preparation, but it will also produce the **outward look of occupation.** Luke 19:13: *"And he called his ten servants, and delivered them ten pounds, and said unto them, Occupy till I come."* Romans 13:11–12: *"And that, knowing the time, that now it is high time to awake out of sleep: for now is our salvation nearer than when we believed. The night is far spent, the day is at hand: let us therefore cast off the works of* *darkness, and let us put on the armour of light."* One would think that the closer we get to the Second Coming, the more God's people would be involved in pointing others to Jesus Christ. That seems logical, but is it that way today?

I believe that the greatest paradox in the Bible is Matthew 24:12: *"And because iniquity shall abound, the love of many shall wax cold."* Does it not seem that when iniquity is abounding, the love of many would wax hot? However, is that true today? There has never been a day in the history of the church of Jesus Christ when we have been taken up by materialism as we are today. God says that the closer we get to the Second Coming, we ought to realize that material things are only a vehicle for doing the will of God. For the past fifty years, I have likely preached an average of twice a day and traveled thousands and thousands of miles. Honestly, many times my wife and I get up in the morning, and it takes several minutes to remember where we are. I have preached while I had the flu and a temperature of 103 degrees. I have preached when on crutches. I have preached with a patch over my eye. Do you know why I do that? Because I believe that Jesus is coming soon. We do not have much time to win people to Christ. Our message is urgent! Sadly, most Christians are fiddling while Rome is burning.

If Jesus is coming soon, why are we so taken up with material possessions? As God has given me the privilege to travel in many countries around the world to preach the Gospel, I have noted that the more a country is like America—the more westernized the culture—the less spiritual results we reap in that country. The more that the people get taken up with a material world, the less spiritual fruit is reaped. We see far more people saved when we go to a primitive or third-world country. That is where the people are hungry for the Gospel because they have not been lulled to sleep in the lap of materialism.

I am quite certain that the reason the number of young people going away to Bible colleges to prepare for ministry is declining is that we as parents have showered everything materially upon our children, and they will not consider laying their luxuries aside for the work of God. Spiritual things are not exciting to them. I remember preaching in Garland, Texas. One young man in that school would not listen to anything that I said. I tried every way in the world to get him to look at me and listen, but he refused. He was totally disinterested. After the chapel service was over, the pastor came to me and said, "Ron, do you know why that young man doesn't listen to you, nor anyone else who preaches in our chapel? His parents gave him a brand new BMW automobile on his 16th birthday, and not one thing spiritual interests him." If his parents are saved, I fear that they will rue the day that they ever gave him that BMW automobile. We need to be teaching our children that there is nothing more important in life than serving the God of Heaven!

A young lady came forward in Tucson, Arizona, to surrender her life to do the will of God. Her Christian mother said, "Oh, Honey, I am so disappointed in your decision tonight. You've given your life tonight for full-time Christian service. What a waste! You know I have always wanted a career for you. Bible colleges are **SO** inferior. I'm so disappointed with your decision tonight." God pity that Christian parent!

Parent, may I ask you, when is the last time you got down on your knees and said, "O God, call my children into Your service." Do you know why the days of fearless Gospel preachers are gone? It is because the day of praying mothers has long since gone. I challenge every parent to promise God that today you will begin to daily pray, "O God, thrust my children into Your harvest fields of service."

When we were in Kenya, Africa, in the mid-1970's, the missionary said, "Brother Comfort, I have been here for thirteen years and when out witnessing, I have never had one door closed in my face. I have never seen a person refuse a gospel tract. Just last year we distributed five million tracts, just our local church alone. If you go down the streets of Nairobi or any other place in Kenya, you need only take a handful of tracts and throw them out the window of your vehicle. The Kenyans will swarm to them like flies swarm to sugar. You talk about liberty to preach. I can go into both the junior and senior high schools, as well as the grade schools, and I can preach and give an invitation with no strings attached."

I will never forget an incident that happened the second time we were in Kenya. Mel Reed, a Canadian pastor and close friend was with us as we were having a week of revival services at Thika Road Baptist Church in Nairobi. Some men from the military came and asked if we could come to have a service for their military unit. I said, "We would be glad to. Is there any time that you could schedule the meeting so that it would not conflict with the services already scheduled here at the church?" He said, "No, I am sorry, but the men convene on Thursday night, and that is the one night they have the time available." I then said, "Well, Brother Mel, you are not preaching in the meeting here at the church. Would you go to the military base?" He said, "I would be glad to go." That night when he returned from the meeting at the military base, I have never seen Mel Reed so excited in all my life. Pastor Reed is typically never at a loss for words, but he could not stand still, and he could not talk straight. He said, "I am not an evangelist, but I preached tonight, and over one hundred—over one hundred received Jesus Christ as their Lord and Savior!"

The military personnel then came back to us and said, "We would like to have another service! We really need to have another service at the military base." So the next week the entire team went out for the meeting. The person in charge said, "There will likely not be quite as many attending this time as many have gone home for the weekend, but I really wanted to have another service." That night, I had the joy of preaching to about 400 military people. At least seventy-five of them came forward that night for salvation. That meant that 175 adults trusted Christ in two services. What am I saying? There are people out there that are hungry for the Gospel, but few will go to tell them.

You can take your fine automobiles and fancy houses. I will choose a grass hut in the will of God any day. I am saddened to know that the work of Jesus Christ around the world in needy and fertile mission fields is severely limited by the lack of money and manpower. If Jesus is coming again soon, we ought to say, "Here is my life, Lord; I am going to invest it in Your service."

The Rapture is a Separating Event.

In I Thessalonians 4:16, the latter part of the verse, we read, "... *and* **the dead in Christ** *shall rise first: Then we which are alive and remain shall be caught up together with them in the clouds..."* Notice the qualifying phrase in that verse: "in Christ." Are you in Christ? For the first seven years of my life, I was in the Roman Catholic Church. For the next eight years of my life, I was in a Southern Baptist Church, but I was as lost as a Southern Baptist as I was as a Roman Catholic. For several years, I traveled throughout North Carolina singing for a Southern Baptist Evangelist in his revival meetings. If Jesus had come during those eight years, I would have been left behind. I was not in Jesus Christ. Are you in Jesus Christ?

I preached in Kansas City, Kansas, and a man said to me, "Brother Comfort, three years ago on Easter Sunday morning when you were here, I was saved. May I tell you a story? I had been a deacon in this fundamental Baptist church for fifteen years. As an 11-year-old boy, I made a profession in order to get my dad and mom off my back. For fifteen years, the folks in this church did not know that I was an unsaved deacon. Don't you think it took a lot for me to swallow my pride and to come down an aisle and tell my church that for fifteen years I had been an unsaved deacon?"

I believe with all my heart that if the Rapture were to take place at this moment, there would be parents who would be shocked that they were taken and their children were left behind. There are children who think they are going to hold on to mom's apron strings or dad's coattails when the Rapture comes. It will not happen. Imagine a man and wife in bed together. Jesus may come in the middle of the night. The wife is saved; the man is not. What happens? The wife goes to see Jesus, and the next morning her husband gets up and sees her bedclothes laying unnaturally on the bed. So he goes to the kitchen. "Honey, are you there?" She is not there. He goes to the living room. "Honey, are you in there?" She is not there. Why? She is in Christ. She is gone. He is not in Christ, and thus, is left behind.

Perhaps the most often asked question about prophecy is this: "Will there be any saved in the Tribulation?" Let me answer that question. First of all, let me say that Romans 11:26–27 says that all Israel will be saved. Then Revelation 7:9–17 says that through the preaching of the Jews a multitude of Gentiles, which no man can number, will be saved. However, those saved will not be anyone who has already heard the Gospel of Christ. My reader friend, if you have already heard the way of salvation, you have had your chance. You will not have an opportunity to be saved in the Tribulation period.

You will find this principle in the Word of God: before God sent His judgment, He always sent a prophet to announce that the judgment was coming. When the judgment came, no one who had a chance to repent before the judgment had a probationary period during the judgment. Did anyone have a chance to repent when the floods came on the land? Did anyone in Sodom and Gomorrah have a chance to repent when God Almighty sent fire and brimstone? When God brought plagues on the land of Egypt, did anyone have a chance to repent? You will not have a chance in the Tribulation because you have had your chance now.

Regarding the oft-asked question about whether or not people will be saved in the Tribulation, let me back up my answer with Scripture. II Thessalonians 2:9–12, speaking of the Antichrist, states this: *"Even him, whose coming is after the working of Satan with all power and signs and lying wonders, And with all deceivableness of unrighteousness in them that perish; because they received not the love of the truth, that they might be saved. And for this cause God shall send them strong delusion, that they should believe a lie: That they all might be damned who believed not the truth, but had pleasure in unrighteousness."* Do you see what that means, friend? If Jesus comes today, and you are left behind, your eternal destiny is already settled.

The Rapture is a Sublime Event.

I Thessalonians 4:17 says, *"Then we which are alive and remain shall be caught up together with them in the clouds, to meet the Lord in the air: and so shall we ever be with the Lord."* There are two Greek words for the word translated "air." A man can go to Mount Olympus and stand on that mountain and point upward. One Greek word signifies that the air is above the mountain tops. The man can stand on that same mountaintop and point downward, and he will use a different word to designate the air below the mountaintop.

Do you know where Jesus is coming to get his little children? He is not coming in the air above the mountain tops. He is coming in the air below the mountain tops. This truth is significant in light of Ephesians 2:2 which states that the devil is the *"prince of the power of the air."* Do you know what air Satan rules? He is the prince of the power of the air below the mountaintop. This world is the kingdom of Satan, but one day King Jesus is going to invade Satan's domain. He is going to snatch away His little children, and so shall we ever be with the Lord. We sing the song, "He's Got the Whole World in His Hands." I am sorry, but that song is not true of God and this world. God does not have this wide world in His hands. This is not the kingdom of God. I John 5:19 says that the whole world lies in the hands of the wicked one.

The coming of our Lord for His own is significant for three reasons. First of all, it will mean **a reunion with our loved ones**. Many years ago, my wife carried a baby for over ten months. She had previously had two miscarriages, so as this pregnancy dragged on, we were very apprehensive. I feared that something was not right, and should our baby be born with serious health issues, I wanted to be at home to comfort my wife. I cancelled some meetings and tried to stay close to home, but still our baby did not come. Four years before, I had scheduled a meeting north of Grand Rapids, Michigan, and really felt that I needed to honor that commitment. So I drove from West Virginia to the meeting. The first Sunday night after the service, my mother-in-law called me with sad news. After finally doing an x-ray, the doctor learned that our baby had a serious neurological defect and would not live. My wife was not told the outcome of the x-ray, so she did not yet know that our daughter would not live. The doctor planned to take the baby by C-section the following morning. I immediately got in my car and began the long drive back to West Virginia so that I would arrive before the baby was delivered. However, my wife went into labor and our baby girl was born at 3 a.m. I did not arrive until 6 o'clock. Our Rachel Jan lived for only ten minutes and then God took her to be with Himself. My wife carried Rachel Jan for ten and one-half months. She never got to touch her; she never got to see her; she never got to hold her. As I stood by the grave of my little daughter, and my pastor read I Corinthians 15:51–58, those verses never meant as much to me in my life as they did that day. As I stood there, in my heart I said, "Rachel, honey, I love you with all of my heart. I have never seen you, but on the way up, when Jesus comes, I am going to tell you that I love you."

One of the greatest times of my life was when my daughters were small and after returning to our RV after an evening service, they would put on their pajamas and then run and jump on me squealing, "Daddy, it's love time! It's love time!" We would hug and kiss and roll around on the floor saying, "I love you!" I used to look forward to seeing Robin as a three-year-old "waddler" coming from the nursery. She would find me at the front of the auditorium and wrap her arms around my knees to give me a big hug. Then I would hear her say, "Daddy, I wuv ooo!" When she said those words, I would tingle all over.

Often our trailer sounded just like the Waltons at bedtime. Ronda, our oldest would begin with, "Daddy, I love you. Mommy, I love you. Goodnight, everybody." Then Becky would chime in with, "Daddy, I love you. Mommy, I love you. Goodnight, everybody." Then Robin would say, "Daddy, I love you. Mommy, I love you. Goodnight, everybody." Then sometimes I would hear them whisper a few words, and before I knew it, the routine had begun again! "Daddy, I love you. Mommy, I love you. Goodnight, everybody." After going through the second time, sometimes they would say, "All right now on the count of three, all together. 1-2-3 DADDY, I LOVE YOU. MOMMY, I LOVE YOU. GOODNIGHT EVERYBODY!" Never one time in all of my life was I ever tempted to say, "Would you SHUT UP and go to sleep?!?!" Never one time! Oh I loved it.

When we lived in West Virginia, every time I was home from meetings, I would go by that cemetery out in the country where our baby girl was buried. Even now, when my wife and I travel through that area, we still stop by that country cemetery, and always I say in my heart, "Rachel, honey, it will not be long now." How I anticipate that **reunion with our loved ones.**

Secondly, the return of Christ for His own will also mean **the redemption of our bodies.**

I Corinthians 15:49 states, *"And as we have borne the image of the earthy, we shall also bear the image of the Heavenly."* Philippians 3:21: *"Who shall change our vile body, that it may be fashioned like unto his glorious body…"* Romans 8:23: *"…even we ourselves groan within ourselves, waiting for the adoption, to wit, the redemption of our body."* I am very much aware that many people seldom ever enjoy a good eight hours of sleep at night. In fact, it may have been years since you have slept through the night. You may go to bed at night taking aspirins to soothe your arthritis. You may have some chronic illness or suffer from migraine headaches.

However, in spite of the pain that you may now suffer, I encourage you to rejoice in this fact: the moment you see Jesus, you are going to know the joy of living in a body that is totally incapable of experiencing any type of pain. That body will be just like Jesus—all but the nail prints, and they belong to Him alone.

Many years ago I preached at Calvary Baptist Church in Normal, Illinois, for the first time. I had heard so much about the sweet testimony of Marilyn Wenigar, the pastor's wife, who was diagnosed with MS while still quite young. When I went to the meeting the first time, I would watch Marilyn come in each night on a walker. Every step she took was difficult for her, and her life was filled with suffering. Night after night as I saw her, I could not help but think, "Marilyn, if Jesus Christ comes tonight, that walker is all going to be in the past." The second time I was in her church, she could not attend every night, and when she did come, she was confined to a wheelchair. Honestly, I never saw Marilyn wheeled into that building at night but what I would think, "Marilyn, if Jesus Christ comes tonight, that wheel chair is going to be history." The third time I was at Calvary Baptist Church, Marilyn could not come to the services at all. She could not come in a walker. She could not come in a wheel chair. She was confined to bed, and her husband had to assist her with even the simplest of everyday functions. However, every night when I would preach, Marilyn would have the phone by her ear listening to the services over the telephone. I never preached but what I thought, "Marilyn, if Jesus Christ comes tonight, that MS is all going to be in the past, and you are going to have a body just like Jesus."

Thirdly, the Rapture will also mean **the revelation of Jesus Christ.** Years ago as I was preaching in Indiana, just before the evening message, the pastor asked for a few minutes of testimonies. He specifically asked folks, "Why are you looking forward to going to Heaven?" I remember as though it were last night that a big burly man stood up and said, "Ladies and gentlemen, I am looking forward to going to Heaven because I have a praying mother in Heaven tonight. She prayed years for my salvation and went to be with the Lord before I ever got saved. When I get to Heaven I am going to run down the streets of gold, wrap my arms around my mother's neck, and say, 'Thank you, Mother. Thank you for praying for me.'" He sat down, and a woman stood and said, "Pastor, no one in this building knows the vacuum in my life since God saw fit to take my child. You remember standing at the graveside of my little baby. The thing I look forward to most in Heaven is seeing my precious baby once again." After she sat down, a man stood and said, "Pastor, you know that every Wednesday night I request prayer for my prodigal son. Only God knows how many times I have gone to bed weeping and tossing and turning over my prodigal son. Pastor, to me the most wonderful thing about Heaven is that there will be no heartache there. There will be no sorrow. There will be no prodigal sons there."

As I sat on the platform that evening, I sat there with a heavy heart. In ten minutes of testimonies, not one person stood and said, "I want to go to Heaven because I want to see Jesus." My friend, I do not care about the fine mansions. I do not care about the streets of gold. I want to go to Heaven because I want to see Jesus Christ.

Fanny Crosby, the greatest songwriter the church has ever had, was blinded at the age of six months old. She never liked to be reminded of her blindness. One day when she was well up in years, D.L. Moody was talking to her and said, "Miss Crosby, if you had one desire of your life fulfilled before you breathed your last breath, what would it be?" He said that he knew with all of his heart that she would say, "Mr. Moody, I would just like to see a ray of sunshine." But she did not say that. Instead, she said, "Mr. Moody, if I had one desire of my life fulfilled, it would be that I would remain blind until I breathe my last breath so that the first person to gladden my eyes would be the Son of God Himself." No wonder this great songwriter could write,

> "I want to see my Savior first of all,
> Before on any others I would call.
> And then for countless days, on His dear face I'll gaze.
> I want to see my Savior first of all."

> "When my life's work is ended, and I cross the swelling tide,
> And the bright and glorious morning I shall see.
> I shall know my Redeemer when I reach the other side
> And His smile will be the first to welcome me.

> "I shall know Him. I shall know Him.
> And redeemed by His side I shall stand.

I shall know Him. I shall know Him,
By the prints of the nails in His hands."

Do you know who wrote that song? Fanny Crosby.

Last Things

Chapter 2
The Judgment Seat of Christ

I Corinthians 3:11–15:

> *For other foundation can no man lay than that is laid, which is Jesus Christ.*
> *Now if any man build upon this foundation gold, silver, precious stones, wood, hay, stubble;*
> *Every man's work shall be made manifest: for the day shall declare it, because it shall be revealed by fire; and the fire shall try every man's work of what sort it is.*
> *If any man's work abide which he hath built thereupon, he shall receive a reward.*
> *If any man's work shall be burned, he shall suffer loss: but he himself shall be saved; yet so as by fire.*

This perhaps is the most classic passage in all of the New Testament on what is commonly termed the Judgment Seat of Christ. The next thing on God's prophetic calendar is the Rapture of the church. Soon Jesus is coming in the air, and those of us who are saved will be raised to meet Him. Immediately, we will find ourselves standing at the Judgment Seat of Christ.

When I was a college student, somehow I imagined in my mind that the Judgment Seat of Christ was comparable to a Sunday school picnic. I thought that just as those who are victorious in the different contests and games played throughout the picnic get a blue ribbon, and those who are not victorious do not get a blue ribbon, it is not such a big deal! Thus, I thought that at the Judgment Seat of Christ, if I get a blue ribbon, that will be fine; if I do not get a blue ribbon, at least I will be saved. Most people commonly believe that at the Judgment Seat of Christ, those who are faithful will get a reward, and those who are not faithful will not be rewarded. That is what I call an academic view of the Judgment Seat of Christ. Academia is filled with this spiritually anemic attitude about the Judgment Seat of Christ. If that concept is true—if this is an apt description of the Judgment Seat of Christ—then it is contrary to the nature of God. God is holy; therefore, the Judgment Seat of Christ must be in keeping with the nature of God.

Secondly, if this flippant, light attitude that I described is true, then it is in definite contrast and contradiction to an age of justice. We now live in an age of grace. I deserve the same thing that you deserve—an eternal hell; and everything that you and I get now is by grace. Jonah 2:9: *"Salvation is of the LORD."* It is His grace that brought me safe thus far, and grace will lead me home. However, when we stand at the Judgment Seat of Christ, that is no longer an age of grace, but it will be an age of justice. At the Judgment Seat of Christ rewards will not be distributed simply because we are Christians. Because this event will take place in an age of justice, whatever is received at the Judgment Seat of Christ will have been earned because of faithfulness as a child of God.

In 1966, my wife and I were in Grand Rapids, Michigan, and had the privilege to attend an International World Fundamental Baptist Congress. I was in the very early years of my ministry, and I thank God that I heard Dr. Robert W. Ketcham preach a message on the Judgment Seat of Christ that revolutionized my thinking on the subject. His message was different than anything that I had ever heard in academia. It stirred my curiosity to do an in-depth study of the Judgment Seat of Christ, and in my study I found, much to my surprise, that only in this generation has the church taken a light view of the Judgment Seat of Christ. No other generation has taken a light view of the Judgment Seat of Christ. I am convinced that our churches are in their current sad condition because of the flippant attitude that we have of the Judgment Seat of Christ. "If I get a reward, fine; if I do not get a reward, no big deal!" I am convinced that the ministry is filled with immorality because of the light view that we have of the Judgment Seat of Christ.

I am also absolutely persuaded that a light view of the Judgment Seat of Christ will produce a light view of sin. Many years ago, I became convinced of this maxim: any doctrine or philosophy that makes it easier for a Christian to sin is not Bible doctrine. I heard a world famous Bible teacher make this statement: "At the Judgment Seat of Christ, everybody is going to be a winner. There will be no losers at the Judgment Seat of Christ." Do you believe that? If that is true, then Demas, who turned back from walking with God, will have an equal standing with the apostle Paul at the Judgment Seat of Christ. If that is true, the Sunday-morning Christian will have an equal standing with Nate Saint, the missionary who was martyred in Quito, Ecuador, for the cause of Christ. If that is true, then the apostle Paul and the Christian who is living in adultery will have an equal standing at the Judgment Seat of Christ. I cannot accept that.

When I heard that statement by the world-famous Bible teacher, I thought to myself, "What motivation is there to live for Christ in that philosophy?" This is motivation: Daniel Webster said, "The most awesome fact of my life is my personal accountability to Jesus Christ." William Graham Scroggie, a Bible teacher of years gone by, said, "I would rather go through the Great Tribulation than to stand at the Judgment Seat of Christ as a carnal Christian." That is motivation.

We will look at three words from the text passage of Scripture to interpret this judgment.

A Day of Revealing

I Corinthians 3:13: *"Every man's work shall be made manifest: for the day shall declare it, because it shall **be revealed** by fire; and the fire shall try every man's work of what sort it is."* The Judgment Seat of Christ will be a day of revealing. II Corinthians 5:10: *"For we must all appear before the judgment seat of Christ; that every one may receive the things done in his body, according to that he hath done, whether it be **good or bad**."* Some say that the word "bad" in the Greek language simply means "useless." If that is the meaning of the word, then the word "good" would likely mean "useful." They are in contrast; they are in contradistinction. Far beyond merely being useless, I believe there is a moral quality to the word "bad." Not only will the good be revealed at the Judgment Seat of Christ, but the bad will also be revealed.

Paul goes on in II Corinthians 5:11 and says, *"Knowing therefore the terror of the Lord, we persuade men; but we are made manifest unto God; and I trust also are made manifest in your consciences."* The word "manifest" means that we will be revealed as we are. We see only the exterior of people, but God sees us as we truly are. When I stand at the Judgment Seat of Christ, I will be revealed as I am. Think on it! A lady came to me one night and said, "Brother Comfort, I am not afraid to stand before the Lord." I said, "Ma'am, that statement is the height of presumption." The apostle Paul could not say that. When Paul thought about standing before the Judgment Seat of Christ, he thought about the terror of the Lord. His attitude was not, "If I get a reward, fine; if I don't get a reward, no big deal!" When he thought about being revealed as he truly was, he felt a terror in his heart.

Not only will the good be revealed, but the bad will be revealed also. Colossians 3:23–25: *"And whatsoever ye do, do it heartily, as to the Lord, and not unto men; Knowing that of the Lord ye shall receive the reward of the inheritance: for ye serve the Lord Christ.* (That is one side of the issue.) *But he that doeth wrong shall receive for the wrong which he hath done:* (That is the other side of the issue.) *and there is no respect of persons."* I contend to you that not only will the good be revealed, but also the bad will be revealed. Not only will the right be revealed, but also the wrong will be revealed at the Judgment Seat of Christ. I Corinthians 4:5: *"Therefore judge nothing before the time, until the Lord come, who both will bring to light the hidden things of darkness, and will make manifest the counsels of the hearts* (revealed as we are): *and then shall every man have praise of God."* The hidden things of darkness will be revealed at the Judgment Seat of Christ.

Romans 14:10–12: *"But why dost thou judge thy brother? Or why dost thou set at nought thy brother? For we shall all stand before the judgment seat of Christ. For it is written, As I live, saith the Lord, every knee shall bow to me, and every tongue shall confess to God. So then every one of us shall give account of himself to God."* It is clearly evident from these verses that when we stand at the Judgment Seat of Christ, we will give a narrative of our Christian life. We are going to tell the Lord Jesus what we did and why we did it. I am convinced that the child of God will confess sin. It will either be confessed now, or while we give our narrative, it will be confessed at the Judgment Seat of Christ. At that day, I am going to tell the Lord Jesus the places I allowed my feet to go. I am going to tell Him the things I permitted my eyes to look upon. I am going to tell Him the things I allowed my hands to do. I am going to tell Him what I did and why I did it as a child of God. What a thought!

Years ago, a preacher told me that when he was a little boy, he had stolen from a man who highly respected him. His daddy came home from work and found out that his son had stolen. He called his boy to him and said, "Son, I heard about you. I heard that you are a thief. We are going to do two things. Number one, I am going to give you a spanking. No son of mine is going to grow up to be a thief. Number two, you and I are going to go before the man from whom you stole, and you are going to tell him that you are a thief." The young boy said, "Daddy, I don't mind the licking, as I deserve that. But please don't make me go before that man and tell him that I am a thief." He said, "Son, whether you want to or not, you are going to do it." This pastor said that he never felt the whipping while he was being whipped, but the hardest thing that he had ever done in his entire life was to stand before that man and tell him that he was a thief.

Our churches are filled with Christians who are totally useless to the cause of Christ because of a bitter, critical spirit. Others go through life with a chip on their shoulder and an unforgiving attitude against another Christian brother, and they are too proud to confess their faults and get it right. There is coming a day in which all those wrongs will be made right. You will make it right at the very Judgment Seat of Christ Himself when the hidden things of darkness will be revealed.

There are two days in the New Testament that sometimes are equated, but I personally do not believe they are the same. First of all, there is the Day of the Lord, and secondly, there is the Day of Christ. I believe that the Day of the Lord refers to the judgments of God upon the world and upon the Jewish nation after the Rapture and throughout the Tribulation.

The Day of Christ refers to that day when those of us who are saved stand at the Judgment Seat of Christ. Many statements in Scripture concerning the Day of Christ are truly heart searching. Philippians 1:10: *"That ye may approve things that are excellent;"* (Don't waste your time on things that are good. Strive for the excellent.) *...that ye may be sincere and without offence till the day of Christ;"* That verse suggests that I may be found with offence at the Day of Christ.

Philippians 2:16: *"Holding forth the word of life; that I may rejoice in the day of Christ, that I have not run in vain, neither laboured in vain."* This verse implies that at the Day of Christ I may not rejoice, because I have run in vain and labored in vain, serving God with impure motives. I Corinthians 1:7–8: *"So that ye come behind in no gift; waiting for the coming of our Lord Jesus Christ: Who shall also confirm you unto the end, that ye may be blameless in the day of our Lord Jesus Christ."* These words suggest that I may be found with blame in the Day of Christ. Some may say, "Brother Comfort, are you telling me that there will be punishment at the Judgment Seat of Christ?" Perhaps I should ask you, "What do you mean by punishment?" Punishment to one is not always punishment to the other.

My three daughters are very diverse in personality. If I had ten children, each of them would be uniquely different. The truth of the matter is that there are no two individuals exactly alike on earth, a valid disproof of evolution. Because my daughters were different in personality, I did not always deal with them in exactly the same way. For instance, I could name nothing that my oldest daughter Ronda hated worse than a spanking. When I mentioned the word "spank," she would go into dry heaves and convulsions. I once read an article from the newspaper to her about a judge in North Carolina who gave two juveniles their choice of sentence for a misdemeanor that they had committed. He said, "You can either choose to spend ten days and ten nights in jail or to get a spanking by your father." Both chose to be spanked by their daddy. When I read the article to Ronda, she said, "Daddy, I would rather spend ten days and ten nights in jail." There is nothing I could do to Ronda that would hurt her worse than a spanking.

Our middle daughter, Becky, is a bookworm ultimate. All of our girls love to read, but none could compete with Becky in number of books read. When our girls were growing up, they did not have television; so they learned to play an instrument, to communicate, and to read books. Becky used to read an average of ten books each week. In contrast, before I got saved, I never read a book through. When the teacher would assign a book report, I would read the first and last chapters, and write the report. After God saved me, He gave me a love for reading; but before I was saved, I never read a book completely through. The first thing Becky would want to know when we would pull our RV into town was "Where is the closest library?" When she had five minutes, she would coil up in the corner of the couch with a book in her hand and read. One day I noticed her reading, and I said, "Honey, you love to read, don't you?" She said, "Oh yes, Daddy. I do love to read." I said, "Well, honey, I have noticed that you sometimes read the same books over and over again. Why do you do that?" She said, "I just enjoy them." I asked, "What book have you read more than any other book?" She said, "Probably *Little Women*." I said, "Honey, how many times have you read *Little Women*?" She guessed that probably she had read that same book about twenty times. I said, "Becky, if you had been naughty, and I gave you a choice of either taking your books away from you for one week or giving you a spanking, what would you choose?" She said, "Daddy, there is nothing that you could do to me that would hurt me worse than taking my books away from me for one week."

On the other hand, our youngest daughter, Robin, loved her dollies. By the way, it has been amazing to me how much college girls love their dollies! In the first year of Ambassador Baptist College, a girl brought thirteen stuffed animals to college with her. Her roommate got out of the upper bunk bed, stepped on one of the stuffed animals, twisted her ankle and had to be on crutches for a few days. Consequently, we had to put a rule in our handbook that no girl (or boy) could bring more than three stuffed animals into their dorm room. As Robin was approaching her fifth birthday, my wife made her a doll that was exactly as tall as Robin. Please remember that we lived in a 40-foot fifth wheel RV. My wife vows that I saw that monstrous doll before the day of her unveiling, but I do not remember seeing it. When the doll was given to Robin, I said, "Oh, Honey, we don't have room in this trailer for another child!" Amanda was so big that Robin dressed her in her own clothing. Perhaps you are familiar with bunk beds in an RV. They are typically not much wider than a church pew. Robin knew that there was not room in her bunk bed for Amanda, but before she went to sleep at night, she would have Amanda snuggled up close to her. Five minutes after Robin was asleep, Amanda was kicked off the top bunk and spent the night on the floor. But she had to at least begin the night with Amanda snuggled up close to her. One night, I came by her room and I said, "Honey, you love Amanda, don't you?" She said, "Oh yes, Daddy, (kiss, kiss, kiss) I love Amanda!" I said, "Well darling, let me ask you a question. If you had been naughty and Daddy gave you a choice of either getting a spanking or my taking Amanda away from you for a whole week, what would you choose?" Honestly, she grabbed Amanda, and she said, "Oh no, Daddy, (kiss, kiss, kiss) not Amanda (kiss, kiss). Please don't take Amanda!" The worst thing that I could have done to Robin is to take Amanda away from her.

Thus, you see that sometimes my approach to discipline for my daughters was different. I took into account their personalities, their attitudes, and the things that were most precious to them.

When Jesus Christ came out of the Judgment Hall knowing that Peter had betrayed Him three times, did Jesus take the cat-of-nine tails and scourge Peter thirty-nine times? He did not. Rather He cast an accusing glance in the direction of Peter. What did Peter do? He went out and wept bitterly. I believe that if we could ask Peter today, "Peter, would you have rather had thirty-nine lashes with the cat-of-nine tails or the accusing glance of the Son of

41

God." I believe Peter would say, "A thousand times over, I would rather have had the cat-of-nine tails!" When we see Jesus in all of His holiness, in all of His glory, and in all of His purity, I believe that in our narrative at the Judgment Seat of Christ, we will willingly confess all those sins and attitudes and evils that have offended Him. What a thought!

A Day of Rewarding for Some.

I Corinthians 3:14: *"If any man's work abide which he hath built thereupon, he shall receive a reward."* I Corinthians 3:8: *"Now he that planteth and he that watereth are one: and every man shall receive his own reward according to his own labour."* II John 8: *"Look to yourselves, that we lose not those things which we have wrought, but that we receive a full reward."* God desires to reward faithfulness at the Judgment Seat of Christ. However, according to II John 8, it is also possible to lose rewards. It is possible for me right now to drop out on God after all of these years of preaching in evangelism and lose the reward of all my years of service. Not many men in the Bible could come to the end of their life and say, "I have fought a good fight. I have finished my course." Only if we faithfully finish the course that God has planned for us will we be rewarded at the Judgment Seat of Christ. Revelation 22:12: *"And, behold, I come quickly; and my reward is with me, to give every man according as his work shall be."* Matthew 10:42: *"And whosoever shall give to drink unto one of these little ones a cup of cold water only in the name of a disciple, verily I say unto you, he shall in no wise lose his reward."* Ephesians 6:8: *"Knowing that whatsoever good thing any man doeth, the same shall he receive of the Lord,"*

Many have the mistaken idea that only preachers will be rewarded at the Judgment Seat of Christ. That is not true. God is taking note of every layman that comes to a church building and lays a paintbrush to the walls or pounds a nail into the building simply because he loves God. God is aware of every man or teenage boy who mows the grass around the church property or at their pastor's house. Though no one else may know anything about it, God is taking note of every woman who comes to a country church and pushes a vacuum sweeper over the carpets and cleans the bathrooms. Every woman who serves in the nursery with a right attitude will get a reward when she stands at the Judgment Seat of Christ. Some ladies go to the nursery with a poor attitude—"I've got to take care of those BRATS again!" My dear friend, if no one takes care of those "brats," no one will get saved in the auditorium! A better attitude would be, "I may not have the talent to sing in the choir, or to teach a Sunday School class, but I can keep the nursery. That is my service to God." God will reward the faithful service of **every** Christian, not just preachers.

The Bible mentions five crowns by name. Those who have trusted Christ as Savior can by faithfulness to our Lord win one or more of these crowns.

- I Corinthians 9:25–27 states that the **incorruptible crown** is reserved for everyone who is laying up treasures in Heaven and not on earth. 1Corinthians 9:25–27: *"And every man that striveth for the mastery is temperate in all things. Now they do it to obtain a corruptible crown; but we an incorruptible. I therefore so run, not as uncertainly; so fight I, not as one that beateth the air: But I keep under my body, and bring it into subjection: lest that by any means, when I have preached to others, I myself should be a castaway."* The following question will determine whether you are a candidate for this crown: what does money mean to you? You may say, "Brother Comfort, it means I can pay my credit card bills. It means I can have all the nice things I desire." Some will lose rewards at the Judgment Seat of Christ because you are a slave to credit cards. As I preach across the country, many men have sadly said to me, "Brother

Comfort, God has called me to preach, but I can't preach because I am in debt ten thousand dollars to a credit card." By the way, how you handle God's money will reveal what kind of character you have. I have never known a man in the ministry who was promiscuous morally who was not also promiscuous in the handling of his finances. These two evils go hand in hand. The first thing a church should do when considering a new pastor is to check his financial background. How you handle your personal money will also be how you handle money in the house of God. Is your money anything more than a vehicle by which to do the will of God? The incorruptible crown is for those who lay up treasures in Heaven!

- II Timothy 4:8 speaks of the **crown of righteousness**. This crown is reserved for everyone who loves the Second Coming of Christ. II Timothy 4:8: *"Henceforth there is laid up for me a crown of righteousness, which the Lord, the righteous judge, shall give me at that day: and not to me only, but unto all them also that love his appearing."* If you could have one desire of your life fulfilled at this moment, what would it be? If anything is dearer to you than the Second Coming of Christ, you have forfeited your crown of righteousness.

- In I Thessalonians 2:19 the Bible speaks of the **crown of rejoicing**. This is the soul-winners crown. I Thessalonians 2:19–20: *"For what is our hope, or joy, or crown of rejoicing? Are not even ye in the presence of our Lord Jesus Christ at his coming? For ye are our glory and joy."* Can you point to anyone and say, "There goes one of my spiritual children?" The songwriter said, "Just a gate opened wide, and a friend by my side when I come to the end of the road. That is all that I ask as a crown for my task, when I come to the end of the road."

- James 1:12 and Revelation 2:10 speak of the **crown of life**. James 1:12: *"Blessed is the man that endureth temptation: for when* *he is tried, he shall receive the crown of life, which the Lord hath promised to them that love him."* Revelation 2:10: *"Fear none of those things which thou shalt suffer: behold, the devil shall cast some of you into prison, that ye may be tried; and ye shall have tribulation ten days: be thou faithful unto death, and I will give thee a crown of life."* This crown is reserved for anyone who is willing to lay down his or her life for the cause of Christ. To these brave soldiers, their attitude is "God has allowed this trial or difficulty to make me better and not bitter." As I consider this crown, I think not only of those who have been martyred for their faith in Christ, but I think of those who have suffered afflictions with a brave and faithful spirit. I think about Erin who was born with spina bifida and has endured twenty-three surgeries! Yet, never once have I ever heard her complain. She will stand far in front of Ron Comfort at the Judgment Seat of Christ. Do not feel sorry for Erin or for any other one who faces difficulty with the peace of God ruling in his heart. God will amply compensate them at the Judgment Seat of Christ.

- According to I Peter 5:4, there is the **shepherd's crown**. I Peter 5:4: *"And when the chief Shepherd shall appear, ye shall receive a crown of glory that fadeth not away."* This crown is reserved for every pastor who faithfully feeds the flock of God. Pray for your pastor. Be his right hand man. Love him. Protect his calling. Exalt his ministry. However, are you aware that even women can earn the shepherd's crown? The Bible states that if you receive a prophet in the name of a prophet you will get a prophet's reward.

Some may say, "Why would we desire a crown?" Be assured that we are not going to stack them on top of our heads and go all over Heaven bragging about how many crowns we have won! Revelation 4:10 tells us what we will do with our crowns: *"The four and twenty elders fall down before him that sat on the throne, and worship him that liveth for ever and ever, and cast their crowns before the throne.*" That is beautiful! You may wonder, "Brother Ron, are you working for a reward?" Absolutely not! I am working because I love Jesus Christ, and because I love Him, I desire a crown to lay before his nail-pierced feet.

The songwriter said,
  "Must I go and empty-handed?
  Thus my dear Redeemer meet.
  Not one soul with which to greet him,
  Lay no trophy at his feet?"

If Jesus came today, would you have any crowns to place before his feet?

A Day of Remorse for Some

I Corinthians 3:15: "*If any man's work shall be burned, he shall suffer loss: but he himself shall be saved; yet so as by fire.*" This Scripture is commonly interpreted as, "If I get a reward, fine; if I don't get a reward, no big deal, at least I will get to Heaven."

One may enter Heaven in two ways. I John 2:28 states, "*And now, little children, abide in him; that, when he shall appear, we may have confidence, and not be ashamed before him at his coming.*" **You can enter Heaven ashamed.** However, according to II Peter 1:11, **you can have an abundant entrance** into the kingdom of our Lord and Savior Jesus Christ. "*For so an entrance shall be ministered unto you abundantly into the everlasting kingdom of our Lord and Saviour Jesus Christ.*" Which way do you want to enter Heaven?

Imagine that you have lived all of your life with an idea of a dream house. One day an architect draws up the plans for that house. Finally in your later years, you are able to build that dream house, paying a half million dollars to complete it. You furnish your lovely house with the most elaborate, expensive furnishings and accessories that money can buy. But one day a fire burns your dream home to the ground. Everything is reduced to ashes, and you alone are rescued from that fire. You have no insurance to rebuild. Do you think that your attitude would be, "Hey, at least I am saved. No big deal!" Saved, yet so as by fire.

Notice three reasons the Bible gives why some will enter Heaven ashamed.

1. Some will enter Heaven **ashamed because of misused time**. Ephesians 5:15–16: *"See then that ye walk circumspectly, not as fools, but as wise, Redeeming the time, because the days are evil."* That Scripture suggests that if we waste the precious gift of time, we will be ashamed when we stand before God. By the way, I do not like the statement, "Well, I have an hour to kill." You do not have an hour to kill. My dear friend, each moment is a gift from God and one for which you are accountable. God says if you waste time you are a fool. Colossians 4:5: *"Walk in wisdom toward them that are without, redeeming the time."* I Corinthians 7:29: *"But this I say, brethren, the time is short:"* Romans 13:11–12: *"And that, knowing the time, that now it is high time to awake out of sleep: for now is our salvation nearer than when we believed. The night is far spent, the day is at hand: let us therefore cast off the works of darkness, and let us put on the armour of light."* Imagine that throughout your life you have two boxes in your home. Every time that you spend an hour fulfilling the desires of your flesh and for temporal things you write it on a piece of paper and put it in the first box. On the other hand, every time you spend an hour on things that are eternal and truly important, you outline it on a piece of paper and put it in the other box. When you stand at the Judgment Seat of Christ with your two boxes to present to the Son of God, will you be ashamed?

47

Psalm 90:10 says, *"The days of our years are threescore years and ten…"* God does not promise anyone more than seventy years. In Psalm 90:12, He says, *"So teach us to number our days, that we may apply our hearts unto wisdom."* It is interesting that in the Bible, the use of time is generally mentioned in connection with wisdom. If you are wise, you are going to redeem the time, make wise use of it. If you are a fool, you are going to waste time. I read about a preacher who came to the passage in Psalm 90 and said, "I know that God only promises me seventy years." So he multiplied seventy times three hundred sixty-five to determine the number of days God promised. He calculated how many days he had already lived and subtracted that number. Then he made a calendar with sufficient pages for the remaining days that God had promised him. Every day when he came into his office, he would remove another day from that calendar. What does that mean? If Psalm 90:10 is true in my life, I don't have many more days to serve God.

"I have only just a minute,
Only sixty seconds in it,
Forced upon me, can't refuse it,
Didn't seek it, didn't choose it.
But, it is up to me to use it.
I must suffer if I lose it,
Give account if I abuse it,
Just a tiny little minute—
But eternity is in it."
—Dr. Benjamin E. Mays

2. Some will enter Heaven **ashamed because of misplaced treasures.** Matthew 6:19–21: *"Lay not up for yourselves treasures upon earth, where moth and rust doth corrupt, and where thieves break through and steal: But lay up for yourselves treasures in Heaven, where neither moth nor rust doth corrupt, and where thieves do not break through nor steal: For where your treasure*

is, there will your heart be also." What do the clothes you are wearing mean to you? They are simply a vehicle for doing the will of God. Is your automobile your most prized possession? The car that I drive is simply a vehicle for doing the will of God.

In 1996, as we were in the midst of completing the Lattimore campus renovation at Ambassador Baptist College, I walked into my office one morning, and my wife greeted me with these words: "Honey, we were just notified by the bank that we must have $8,000 deposited by two o'clock this afternoon for withholding taxes." We did not have sufficient money to meet this obligation. I had no idea where we could find that amount of money! As I sat down at my desk in despair, I noticed a letter in front of me. The letter was from a married student with a family who commuted about forty miles each day to school. He often did not know how he would make his next school tuition payment. When I opened the letter it read, "Dear Brother Comfort, my wife and I have prayed for a long time that God would supply $10,000 for us to give to Ambassador Baptist College to show our appreciation for what the school has meant in our lives. Three years ago, I had a wreck and my medical expenses were $10,000. Because of a technicality, our insurance company refused payment. However, God supplied the $10,000 by other means, and all the bills are paid. My wife and I were completely surprised a few days ago to receive a check in the mail for $10,000 from the insurance company. We each prayed separately about what we should do with the money. We did not discuss it together for quite some time. When we did sit down to discuss what we should do with the money, both of us concluded that this was the answer to our prayer. We are giving the college $10,000 because of our love for God and in appreciation for what He has done in our lives through

Ambassador Baptist College." I looked at that check, and I wept. I showed the letter to my wife, and after reading it, she too began to weep. She said, "Honey, the dedication of some our students put us to shame." Where are your treasures?

3. Some will enter Heaven **ashamed because of misappropriated talents.** I Corinthians 6:19: *"What? know ye not that your body is the temple of the Holy Ghost which is in you, which ye have of God, and ye are not your own?"* Do you realize that you do not have a right to order your life? Not one of you would go next door to steal from your neighbor. Hopefully, you are not one that would rob a bank or a store. However, you steal from God each day of your life by ordering your own life apart from His plan for you. You have your life all planned out. You know how much money you are going to make. You know what kind of car you are going to drive. You know what kind of house you are going to live in. You know when you will retire and how much money you will have in the bank. But you have never said, "God, what would you have me to do?" The turning point in every person's life should be exactly as the apostle Paul experienced it, *"Lord, what wilt thou have me to do?"* (Acts 9:6)

In 1636, Harvard was founded. From 1636–1791, one-half of the graduates of Harvard went into the ministry. Imagine it, one-half of the graduates entered ministry! There has never been a college in the history of the human race that in over 150 years put half of their graduates into the ministry. Yet Harvard did. In 1701, Yale was founded because some were persuaded that they saw a slippage in Harvard. Yale was founded to be a "true school of the prophets." In 1701, President Thomas Clapp gave this definition of education. "Education is a group of ministers training young people for the service of God." Think of that.

Fast forward to 1981 when one-half of one percent of the students going away to college in the United States were going away to college for the purpose of getting into the ministry and most of that small percentage never entered the ministry. Furthermore, in 1986, from our Christian Liberal Arts Colleges, only fifteen percent of the graduates went into the ministry. When I was at Bob Jones University in the late 1950's and early 1960's, Bob Jones University and Tennessee Temple University had 2,000 preacher boys. Today if we added together the ministerial class enrollment of all fundamental Christian colleges, there would be less than 2,000 preacher boys.

When I pray on Sunday morning for the pastors on my prayer list, I often think that most of the men for whom I pray are in the fifty to sixty age category, or perhaps older. Here is my burden: Where are their replacements? Where are those young men who are willing to stand in the gap and fill the many vacancies in our churches?

Don't be a fool and waste your time on making money. Time is too short. One day soon, we will stand at the Judgment Seat of Christ. Will you be ashamed before Him at His coming? My friend, the first principle of stewardship is this: "Lord I belong to you…lock, stock, and barrel. My life is Yours to control."

Last Things

Chapter 3
The Church in the Book of Revelation

Revelation 1:10–13:

> *"I was in the Spirit on the Lord's day, and heard behind me a great voice, as of a trumpet,*
> *Saying, I am Alpha and Omega, the first and the last: and, What thou seest, write in a book, and send it unto the seven churches which are in Asia; unto Ephesus, and unto Smyrna, and unto Pergamos, and unto Thyatira, and unto Sardis, and unto Philadelphia, and unto Laodicea.*
> *And I turned to see the voice that spake with me. And being turned, I saw seven golden candlesticks;*
> *And in the midst of the seven candlesticks one like unto the Son of man, clothed with a garment down to the foot, and girt about the paps with a golden girdle."*

The Greek word for the word "church" simply means "a called-out assembly" and is used in two ways in the New Testament. In Revelation 1:11, the word "church" refers to seven literal, local churches, called-out assemblies. The vast amount of times when the word is used in the New Testament, it designates a local assembly. On the other hand, you may have heard some Christian people or even preachers speak of an "invisible" church. That term is a contradiction in itself. There has never been a called-out assembly that is invisible. An assembly cannot be invisible. There have to be visible bodies in order for the group to be a called-out assembly. When people speak of the invisible church, they are really referring to the church in prospect: that body of believers that has not yet been completed. Some who are in that body have already died and gone to be with the Lord. Some in that body are currently alive. Those of us who are saved today are part of that body in prospect. However, some in that body will be saved in the future and will comprise in totality the church in prospect.

It is interesting to notice that the word church is used twenty times in Revelation chapters one, two, and three. Every time the word is used, it means a local assembly. Move ahead to the next time the word "church" is used: Revelation chapter twenty-two, verse sixteen. Again, the word "church" refers to local assemblies.

My message in this chapter concerns the church in prospect, **The Church in the Book of Revelation.**

The Church Raptured

In Revelation 4:1–3, John says,

> *"After this I looked, and, behold, a door was opened in Heaven: and the first voice which I heard was as it were of a trumpet talking with me; which said, Come up hither, and I will shew thee things which must be hereafter.*
> *And immediately I was in the spirit: and, behold, a throne was set in Heaven, and one sat on the throne.*
> *And he that sat was to look upon like a jasper and a sardine stone: and there was a rainbow round about the throne, in sight like unto an emerald."*

Notice that John looks up and sees the door. Who is the door? In John 10:9, Jesus says, *"I am the door: by me if any man enter in, he shall be saved, and shall go in and out, and find pasture."* John looks up, sees Jesus, and hears a trumpet. I Thessalonians 4:17 and I Corinthians 15:51 both state that Jesus is coming with the trump of God. I like the second word in Revelation 4:2. He looks up, sees the door, hears the trump, and *"immediately..."*; he is not left behind to go through the Tribulation period. From Revelation chapters six through nineteen, you see the judgments of God poured out upon the earth in the Tribulation period. However, through all these chapters, the church is viewed from a Heavenly viewpoint. We are with our Savior, the Lord Jesus Christ. John is raptured **before** the judgments come upon the earth.

John sees a green rainbow round about the throne. There is a brilliant, resplendent diamond affect emanating from the throne of God. A vibrant red color originates from the throne of God. Why is the rainbow circular? Today we see a semicircular, multi-color rainbow. John did not see a semicircle, but rather a complete circle. Whenever I think of God, I like to think of God as a circle. Where does a circle begin? It has no beginning. Where does a circle end? It has no end. That is God! Micah 5:2 says, *"…whose goings forth have been from of old, from everlasting."* Psalm 90:2 says, *"Before the mountains were brought forth, or ever thou hadst formed the earth and the world, even from everlasting to everlasting, thou art God."* God is from eternity to eternity.

Nothing takes God by surprise. We often speak of accidents, but there are no accidents in a world governed by a sovereign God. God did not look down on September 11, 2001, and say, "Uh-oh, I did not know that was going to happen." The complete circular rainbow reminds me that there are many things about life that I do not know. Many times the devil tempts me to say to God, "Why? Why, God?" Maybe you have stood by the grave of a departed loved one, and Satan tempted you to say, "God, why?" When we get to Heaven, the word "W-H-Y" will be extracted from our vocabulary. We are going to see things as a whole. We are going to see the end from the beginning. We are going to know even as God knows.

I well remember preaching in Peoria, Illinois. A lady brought her beautiful little three-year-old toddler to the platform after the Sunday night message. As I spoke with the mother, I could not help but notice the unusual way her little girl walked. It was heart-rending to watch. The mother said, "Brother Comfort, Why?

Why?" I said, "Ma'am, what do you mean by why?" She said, "My husband is in Bible college. He is studying to preach, and yet, here is my three-year-old daughter stricken with crippling arthritis. Why?" I said, "Ma'am, I do not know why, but I do know this, God has yet to make His first mistake. When he makes His first mistake, He will cease to be God." He knows the end from the beginning. He alone knows all.

This circular rainbow is also a green rainbow and not a multi-colored rainbow. As a rainbow was a promise of grace to Noah, so is this green rainbow. This rainbow is a promise of grace to every child of God. It is a promise of a new age of fertility. One day the deserts are going to bloom with blossoms. The curse will be lifted, and the lion and the lamb are going to lie down in peace together. I believe that this green rainbow prophesies a golden millennial dawn.

The Church Rewarded

Revelation 4:4 says, *"And round about the throne were four and twenty seats* (or *thrones*; it is the same Greek word.): *and upon the seats I saw four and twenty elders sitting, clothed in white raiment; and they had on their heads crowns of gold."* Years ago, I preached that Christians would not be anywhere present at the Great White Throne Judgment. I was taught this in college. However, one day in my studies, I came upon I Corinthians 6:2–3 which says, *"Do ye not know that the saints shall judge the world? …Know ye not that we shall judge angels…"* I began to wonder, "Where are we going to judge angels? Where are we going to judge the world?" I concluded that it may fall to our lot at the Great White Throne Judgment of God to have to pronounce the sentence of a lake of fire on our own unsaved loved ones. Think about that. How would you feel in that day, if you had to pronounce the sentence of the lake of fire on your unsaved son? What if your son looked at you and said, "Daddy, it is your fault that I must suffer this punishment for all eternity. If Jesus Christ had meant more to you on Sunday night than NFL football on television, I might have thought that there was something to Christianity. If you had been more than a Sunday morning Christian, I might have been saved." What an awesome thought it is that those of us who are saved may have to pronounce the sentence of the lake of fire on our own loved ones!

In Revelation four, verse four, we read the number *"twenty-four."* Six times in the Old Testament this number is used, and each time it is in connection with the priestly tribe of Israel. There are those who will say that these twenty-four elders represent the Old and the New Testament saints, i.e. the twelve tribes of Israel and the twelve apostles. It is my conviction that the Old Testament saints are not raised at the Rapture with the Church Age. I believe that the Old Testament saints will be raised along with the Tribulation saints seven years after the Rapture.

Scripture says that these saints have white raiment; they are dressed in priestly garments. Here are twenty-four elders; elders are always representatives. In the Old Testament, sometimes they represented a family, sometimes they represented a tribe, and sometimes they represented a city. Who do these men represent? It is my contention that they represent the church of Jesus Christ. I believe that these twenty-four elders are God's New Testament priests. I Peter 2:5 reads, *"Ye also, as lively stones, are built up a spiritual house, an holy priesthood."* I Peter 2:9 states, *"But ye are a chosen generation, a royal priesthood, an holy nation, a peculiar people;"* Your priesthood means that you do not have to come to Ron Comfort or to any other man to get access to God. You can go into the presence of God for yourself.

These elders are wearing crowns of gold! Some say, "I do not care how I get to Heaven just as long as I get there. That is all that matters to me." That is a cheap definition of Heaven. I truly wonder about the validity of one's salvation who just wants to get to Heaven by the skin of his teeth.

Five crowns are named in the New Testament that every Christian has the opportunity to win. (Read about these crowns in detail in the chapter entitled, "The Judgment Seat of Christ.") What is the purpose of these crowns? Will we stack them on our head and go all over Heaven bragging about how many crowns we have won? Revelation 4:10 states, *"The four and twenty elders fall down before him that sat on the throne, and worship him that liveth for ever and ever, and cast their crowns before the throne."* That is beautiful! If Jesus gives me a crown, I will just lay it right back at His nail-pierced feet. If He came today, would you have any crowns to place before his precious feet?

The Church Rejoicing

Revelation 19:7 says, *"Let us be glad and rejoice, and give honour to him: for the marriage of the Lamb is come, and his wife hath made herself ready."* This is the moment that Jesus Christ has been waiting for from the morn of eternity! He has been waiting for the day when He would be married to His bride. We know who the Lamb is. John the Baptist identified the Lamb in John 1:29 and 36: *"Behold the Lamb of God, which taketh away the sin of the world."*

One day the Lamb will be married. To whom will He be married? Some may say that Israel is the bride because Isaiah chapter fifty-four calls Israel the wife of Jehovah. However, the Bible also says in Jeremiah that Israel played the harlot. Is Jesus going to be married to a harlot? I say not. II Corinthians 11:2 states that He will be married to a chaste virgin. Who is that chaste virgin? If you are saved, that is you; that is I. Preachers frequently say, "We are married to the Son of God!" No! We are not married to Him yet. We are only engaged to Him. Ephesians 1:13 says that when we are saved, we receive *"the seal of the Spirit."* Ephesians 1:14

identifies the seal of the Spirit as "the earnest of the inheritance," i.e. the down payment or the engagement ring. Occasionally, when I return to the college campus after being away to preach a series of evangelistic meetings, some young lady will meet me in the hall and say, "Brother Comfort, while you were gone, I got engaged. Look at my beautiful diamond." I will say, "Why, congratulations! Oh, yes, I **think** I see it." You almost have to have a microscope to find the diamond, but to the prospective bride, it is as big as a mountain. My friends, all we have now is the engagement ring. The wedding is yet to be.

Any married man will admit that he really did not know much about his bride-to-be before the marriage. I used to think that I knew a lot about my sweetheart before I married her, but I did not. I did not know that she had cold feet. I did not know that she would take all of the covers and try to push me out of bed. I did not know that she would think that a king-sized bed was really a single bed, and that I would find myself hanging off the edge. I did not know those things! However, when I got married to her, I started finding out about her, and I must honestly say that the more I find out about her, the more I love her.

One day we will be married to the Son of God. We will swap the engagement ring for a wedding band and will start finding out about Jesus Christ in all His beauty and holiness. I do not know much about Him now. I know that Song of Solomon 5:16 says, *"He is altogether lovely."* I know that David said in Psalm 45:2: *"Thou art fairer than the children of men: grace is poured into thy lips: therefore God hath blessed thee for ever."* I know that David said also in Psalm 89:6: *"For who in the Heaven can be compared unto the LORD? who among the sons of the mighty can be likened unto the LORD?"* I know all of that, but I still do not know much about Jesus because I am only engaged to Him. When I am married to the Son of God, as the eons of eternity roll, I will find out more about Him. And I am absolutely convinced that the more I learn about Him, the more I am going to love Him.

At a wedding, who is the featured person? Without a doubt, the bride is the person of significance. On August 31, 1963, I stood on the platform of a country church. As I looked toward the vestibule, there was my wife-to-be. I am not being irreverent, but I truly mean it. When I looked back there and saw my bride, I said, "Hallelujah! Praise God! Is that the woman that I am going to marry?" I thought that the Rapture had already come. I had never seen anything so beautiful in all of my life. But then I noticed that nobody knew I was there. Everybody was looking at her. All of a sudden, wedding music began to play, and as she walked down the aisle all eyes were fixed on her. I felt like saying, "Hey! I am a part of this, too!" Our engagement was announced about six months before we married. A beautiful picture was published in the newspaper...of HER! It told about her ancestry all the way back to Adam and that she was secretary of the 4-H club, and at the bottom of the column: "P.S. The fellow that she is marrying is Ron Comfort." That is about all they had to say about me. Do you know what? If I had run out of the back door, not a soul would have missed me. Nobody even knew that I was there. The day following our wedding, another beautiful picture was published in the newspaper...of HER! It told about her bridal gown, what her bridesmaids had worn, and at the bottom of the column... "BY THE WAY, the groom was Ron Comfort!"

At a wedding, the bride is always the feature. However, at this Heavenly wedding, the scene will be far different. All eyes are not going to be on the bride, but all eyes will be on the Bridegroom, Jesus Christ. I may look down the row to see one of the guests, John the Baptist, that fiery prophet of God, and I may say, "Hey John, how are you doing?" He may say, "Ron, you keep quiet. I am looking at the Bridegroom, Jesus Christ." I think that I am going to spend the first few thousand years just staring into the face of our lovely Lord.

After a wedding, there is always a honeymoon.

The Church Returning

Revelation 19:11–16 says,

> *"And I saw Heaven opened, and behold a white horse; and he that sat upon him was called Faithful and True, and in righteousness he doth judge and make war.*
> *His eyes were as a flame of fire, and on his head were many crowns; and he had a name written, that no man knew, but he himself.*
> *And he was clothed with a vesture dipped in blood: and his name is called The Word of God.*
> *And the armies which were in Heaven followed him upon white horses, clothed in fine linen, white and clean.*
> *And out of his mouth goeth a sharp sword, that with it he should smite the nations: and he shall rule them with a rod of iron: and he treadeth the winepress of the fierceness and wrath of Almighty God.*
> *And he hath on his vesture and on his thigh a name written, KING OF KINGS, AND LORD OF LORDS."*

The honeymoon begins with a ride on white horses. Who rides the white charger? This warrior is Jesus Christ. Some may say, "That does not sound like sweet baby Jesus!" My reader friend, this is not sweet baby Jesus. The first time He came, He came as a babe; the next time, He is coming as a warrior (Revelation 19:15). When He came the first time, He was laid in a manger; when He comes the next time, He is coming on a white charger (Revelation 19:11). When He came the first time, there was no room in the inn; when He comes the next time, He is going to ask and God will give Him the universe for His inheritance and the uttermost part of the earth for His private possession (Psalm 2:8). When He came the first time, He was *despised and rejected of men*; when He comes the next time, *every knee shall bow and every tongue shall confess that He is Lord to the glory of God the Father* (Philippians 2:9–11). When

He came the first time, a few shepherds beheld His birth; when He comes the next time, *every eye shall see Him and all kindreds of the earth shall wail because of Him* (Revelation 1:7). When He came the first time, a few angels heralded His birth; when he comes the next time, He is coming *with ten thousands of His saints* (Jude 14). When He came the first time, He came in grace; when He comes the next time, He is coming in justice and pure vengeance (II Thessalonians 1:7–8).

Notice with me three things about this entourage. First of all, note that Christ is riding the white charger clothed in *a vesture dipped in blood.* (Revelation 19:13) What is the blood on His vesture? Some have preached that this is the blood of Calvary that saturates His garments; however, at this juncture Jesus is not coming to die on a cross. This is a Warrior coming back to do battle. It is in anticipation of the Battle of Armageddon, World War Number One, which will for the first time involve all nations of the earth. God likens this event to a farmer going into his grape arbor to trample under his feet the harvested grapes. The grape juice splattering against his clean garments turns them red.

> "Mine eyes have seen the glory of the coming of the Lord;
> He is trampling out the vintage where the grapes of wrath are stored;
> He has loosed the fateful lightning of His terrible, swift sword;
> Hallelujah! My God is marching on."

Secondly, take note in Revelation 19:14 of those who accompany Christ on His journey. *"And the armies which were in Heaven followed him…"* Who are these armies? If you are saved, that is you. That is I. Jesus said in John 14:3: *"…that where I am, there ye may be also."* He is on a white charger, and thus I will be with Him on a white charger, too. I Thessalonians 4:17 says, *"…and so shall we ever be with the Lord."* Colossians 3:4 says, *"When Christ, who is our life, shall appear, then shall ye also appear with him in glory."* We will be eyewitnesses at the conclusion of the Battle of Armageddon.

Thirdly, Revelation 19:15 describes the weapon that Christ will use in His battle. *"And out of his mouth goeth a sharp sword, that with it he should smite the nations."* Many prophecy speakers teach that the world will be destroyed by nuclear weapons. Does God really need nuclear weapons? Did He need any instrument to create the universe? No! He spoke the worlds into existence! He said, "Let there be light" and there was light. Creation exists by the Word of God alone.

Isaiah 11:4 explains that at this juncture in the final war of the ages, God will slay the wicked with the breath of His lips. If you are unsaved and the Rapture takes place, your eternal destiny is already sealed. In the film *Left Behind*, the unsaved pilot and his daughter trust Christ as Savior in the Tribulation period. That may make for a good story, but it is not truth. The truth is that one of three things will happen to every unsaved person that goes into the Tribulation:

1. He may be slain by the plagues in the Tribulation.

2. His blood may flow at the War of Armageddon.

3. He will be cast bodily into Hell at the Judgment of the Nations before the millennial reign of Jesus Christ.

If Jesus comes today and you are left behind, your day of grace is over.

The Church Reigning

Revelation 20:6: *"Blessed and holy is he that hath part in the first resurrection: on such the second death hath no power, but they shall be priests of God and of Christ, and shall reign with him a thousand years."* Hallelujah! What a honeymoon! All expenses paid by the blood of Jesus Christ.

The Eastern wedding was in three phases. First is a period of betrothal. We would call that engagement. Many times, the bride and the bridegroom never met each other until they met each other at the marriage altar. The engagement was arranged by the father of the bride and the father of the bridegroom. You can imagine the look of astonishment on the faces of some bridegrooms as they came to the altar and gingerly lifted the bride's veil to find the ugliest thing that they had seen in their life. By that juncture of the ceremony, they were stuck! They knew that were going to have to live with that face "until death do them part." I have in my files a newspaper clipping telling of a man in Egypt that had never seen the woman that he was going to marry. He came to the hotel the morning of the ceremony, and when he got one glimpse of the bride, he went up to the balcony and jumped off committing suicide!

The second phase of the wedding is the ceremony itself. Think of this. When God wanted to paint a picture of the relationship of His Son and the church, He chose the most beautiful relationship on earth, that of a husband and wife. Sadly, many times this beautiful picture is destroyed by divorce. When you come to the marriage altar, be absolutely convinced that you have no other option but "until death us do part."

Thirdly, there was the wedding feast. If the parents were of normal, modest means, the feast would last a day or two. If they were somewhat wealthy, the feast might last a week or two. Our engagement was made by God the Father and God the Holy Spirit before the dawn of Creation. One day, we will be married to our Heavenly Bridegroom. Our Father owns the cattle on a thousand hills, and thus, our wedding feast is not going to last for a day or for a week. It will last for one thousand years—all expenses paid by the blood of Christ.

The Church Residing

In Revelation 21:1–4, John says,

> *"And I saw a new Heaven and a new earth: for the first Heaven and
> the first earth were passed away; and there was no more sea.
> And I John saw the holy city, new Jerusalem, coming down from God
> out of Heaven, prepared as a bride adorned for her husband.
> And I heard a great voice out of Heaven saying, Behold, the
> tabernacle of God is with men, and he will dwell with them, and they
> shall be his people, and God himself shall be with them, and be their
> God.
> And God shall wipe away all tears from their eyes; and there shall be
> no more death, neither sorrow, nor crying, neither shall there be any
> more pain: for the former things are passed away."*

In Genesis chapter three, we read of paradise lost. In Revelation
chapters twenty-one and twenty-two, we see paradise regained. In
those verses, we read of a new Heaven, a new earth, a new people,
a new light, a new temple, and a new city.

In that city, there will be no more sin. Thank God that on the
streets of gold in Heaven there will be no prostitutes, no explicit
movie ads, no drug dealers, and no gay rights movement. Nothing
that defiles will enter into that city, and thus, there will be no more
sin.

Secondly, there will be no more sickness. Many people live each
day in a body throbbing with pain. Many suffer sleepless nights
because of pain or illness. I thank God that once we breathe
celestial air and our feet step on celestial soil, we will realize that
we are living in a body that is totally incapable of experiencing
any type of pain.

Heaven will know no sorrow. There will be no mothers weeping
at the gravesite of precious babies. Broken-hearted parents who
have prayed over prodigal children, weeping in the midnight
hours until there were no more tears to shed, will weep no longer.

In Heaven, there will be no more separation: no graveyards, no funeral processions. Death will be unknown.

Heaven has no sea. Think of that. When the Apostle John wrote the book of the Revelation, he was on the Isle of Patmos. He was exiled to that barren place because of his testimony for Christ. The sea was significant to John, because it was the sea that separated him from the people that he had pastored in Ephesus for twenty to thirty years, people that he loved. I have preached in military churches in many far away countries and have seen thirty-year-old captains sit down and weep because their wives and their children were across the sea. Sea in the Bible is a picture of heartache, and Heaven will know no heartache.

I like to imagine what the city will be like. The Bible gives us some description, but our finite minds sometimes have difficulty visualizing the scene. The city will be foursquare. It will be 1,500 miles long, 1,500 miles wide, and 1,500 miles high. If you have ever flown across the country or over the Pacific or Atlantic Oceans, you know that everything looks so miniscule from the plane's altitude. A huge ship or even a skyscraper looks like a tiny speck. Yet in today's planes, we are traveling only six or seven miles above the earth's surface. Many times I have thought as I have flown, "I wonder what a city 1,500 miles high will be like." The base of that city would stretch from Boston, Massachusetts, to Miami, Florida. It would reach as far west as Dallas, Texas, encompassing two-thirds of the area of the United States. Someone calculated that if there were fifteen feet per story, (I do not know if there will be stories, but God is making it tall for some reason.) there would be 528,000 stories. Every story would be 2¼ million square miles—15,000 times the size of London, England. But, this new city is only a city like Charlotte is a city in North Carolina.

The Bible says that the foundations of that city will be garnished with precious stones: blue stones, green stones, orange stones, diamond-colored stones, purple stones—God is a lover of beauty. Do you love to see a rainbow in the sky after a spring shower? One of the most fascinating things about Hawaii to me is that almost everyday without fail, you will see a rainbow. Sometimes you will see one rainbow over another rainbow. The last time that I was in Hawaii I said to my wife, "Honey, do you know that we have not yet seen a rainbow during our entire time here?" Before that day was over, we saw a triple rainbow! It was breathtaking. However, what is a rainbow good for? You cannot eat it. You cannot wear it. You cannot do anything with it. It certainly is pretty to look at though. God is a lover of beauty. We are going to be surrounded by beauty as the eons of eternity roll.

The Bible says that there will be twelve gates, each gate of one pearl. Could these gates be anything else but pearl? A pearl is the object of suffering. An oyster is continuously pumping, pumping, pumping. One day the oyster gets a grain of sand in its side, and the grain of sand rubs a sore because of the friction of that pumping motion. So the oyster secretes a substance to cover that grain of sand, and that grain of sand becomes a precious pearl. The pearl is the object of a wounded side. I believe that when we walk down streets of gold and gaze on gates of pearl, we are going to be reminded that we are there only because of the wounded side of Jesus Christ.

The Bible tells us that the gates of the city will never be closed so that *"Whosoever will let him come."* They will come from the east and the west and sit down with Abraham, Isaac, and Jacob in the Kingdom of God. Someone may say, "Brother Comfort, will I know my loved ones over there?" Certainly, you know them now. Do you not think that you will know much more over there than you do here? In 1972, I stood by the grave of our precious baby daughter that my wife carried for more than ten months. We never got to hold Rachel Jan. We never got to touch her or even see her. However, when I get to glory, nobody is going to have to introduce me to Rachel Jan. The moment that I see her, I will know her.

Many years ago, in a church in southeast Alabama, a bashful young man named Henry came to his pastor and said, "Pastor, I do not feel that I have done much to serve the Lord. I am ashamed that I have not done more. Is there something that I can do around the church to serve the Lord?" The pastor said, "Henry, would you like to be an usher?" He said, "Pastor, do you mean that? Can I usher in the church?" The pastor said, "Next Sunday, you take your place with the ushers, and they will instruct you." Sunday came, and everyone commented about how happy Henry looked as he ushered people to their pews. A couple of years passed, and Henry was taken with a fatal illness. The pastor visited Henry and said, "I think I know the answer to this question, but I must ask you. Henry, you know that you do not have much time. Where are you going when you leave this life?" Henry said, "Oh pastor, I settled that a long time ago. I know that I am saved. I have no doubt in my mind about that. Pastor, would you do me a favor? Would you read my favorite portion of Scripture? You know what it is." The Pastor turned to Revelation chapter twenty-one and read,

> *"And I saw a new Heaven and a new earth: for the first Heaven and the first earth were passed away; and there was no more sea. And I John saw the holy city, new Jerusalem, coming down from God out of Heaven, prepared as a bride adorned for her husband. And I heard a great voice out of Heaven saying, Behold, the tabernacle of God is with men, and he will dwell with them, and they shall be his people, and God himself shall be with them, and be their God. And God shall wipe away all tears from their eyes; and there shall be no more death, neither sorrow, nor crying, neither shall there be any more pain: for the former things are passed away."*

As the pastor looked up, he noticed big crocodile tears streaming down Henry's face. The pastor took out his handkerchief to wipe the tears away. Henry's dying words were these: "Pastor, the next time those tears are wiped away, Jesus will do it for me in the New Jerusalem." Praise God! How I look forward to that day!

I stood in Duke University hospital in January, 1964, and the nurse said to me, "Ron, one day you may be blind. Because of the eye disease you have, one day your wife may have to read to you, drive for you, and be your eyes." I said, "One day, ma'am, I will have a new pair of eyes, and even then, God will wipe away all tears."

> There's a land beyond the river,
> That we call the sweet forever
> And we only reach that shore by faith's decree.
> One by one we'll gain the portals,
> There to dwell with the immortals;
> When they ring those golden bells for you and me.

Praise God! That is where I am heading. How about you?

Last Things

Chapter 4
The Second Advent

Revelation 19:11–16:

And I saw Heaven opened, and behold a white horse; and he that sat upon him was called Faithful and True, and in righteousness he doth judge and make war.
His eyes were as a flame of fire, and on his head were many crowns; and he had a name written, that no man knew, but he himself.
And he was clothed with a vesture dipped in blood: and his name is called The Word of God.
And the armies which were in Heaven followed him upon white horses, clothed in fine linen, white and clean.
And out of his mouth goeth a sharp sword, that with it he should smite the nations: and he shall rule them with a rod of iron: and he treadeth the winepress of the fierceness and wrath of Almighty God.
And he hath on his vesture and on his thigh a name written, KING OF KINGS, AND LORD OF LORDS.

This passage of Scripture details the Second Advent of Christ.

In I Peter 1:11, Peter describes what the Old Testament saint saw as he looked into the future. *"Searching what, or what manner of time the Spirit of Christ which was in them did signify, when it testified beforehand the sufferings of Christ, and the glory that should follow."* According to Peter when the Old Testament saint looked out into the future, he saw two mountain peaks. The first mountain peak was the suffering of the Messiah. Beyond that mountain peak, he saw another mountain peak, which was the kingdom of the Messiah. As a matter of fact, some Jewish scribes thought that there would be two Messiahs: one that would come and suffer according to Psalm 22 and Isaiah 53, and another Messiah that would come to reign as king according to hundreds of Old

Testament prophecies. These scribes did not understand that this was one and the same Messiah. They saw the two mountain peaks, but they did not see the valley between the two mountain peaks. That valley is called the Church Age.

Colossians 1:26 states that the church was a *"mystery which hath been hid from ages and from generations, but now is made manifest to his saints:"* When the Bible talks about a mystery, it does not mean something that cannot be understood, but it simply means something that has not previously been revealed. The Old Testament saint knew nothing about the Church Age. One day, the last person to complete the body of Christ, the church, will be saved. I never talk about this but what I think, "It could be today!" The last person to complete that body will be saved and then we will hear the shout, the voice of the archangel, and the trump of God and we will go to meet Jesus in the Rapture.

Some people that have been saved for years are not aware of this simple truth. The Second Coming of Christ is in two phases. When He comes for those of us who are saved, His feet will not touch the earth. We will be raised to meet Him in the air. That is called the Rapture. Some may object and say, "Where do you find the word "rapture" in your English Bible?" You will recall from our previous message that the word "rapture" is a transliteration of the Latin word "rapto." I Thessalonians 4:17: *"...caught up together with them in the clouds, to meet the Lord in the air:"* Following the Rapture, Earth will experience the seven years of the Tribulation period. After the seven-year Tribulation, Jesus is coming back to Earth. Those of us who are saved are coming back to Earth with Him. This coming of Christ to Earth is called the Revelation, or the Second Advent.

There are several differences between the Rapture and the Revelation. The Rapture is secret. He is coming **for** His saints. The Revelation is public. He is coming **with** His saints. Revelation 1:7:

"Behold, he cometh with clouds; and every eye shall see him..." That
is the Revelation. Jude 14: *"And Enoch also, the seventh from Adam,
prophesied of these, saying, Behold, the Lord cometh with ten thousands
of his saints."* The Rapture is a message of comfort. I Thessalonians
4:18 says, *"Wherefore comfort one another with these words."* The
Revelation is a message of judgment. II Thessalonians 1:7–8 says,
*"And to you who are troubled rest with us, when the Lord Jesus shall
be revealed from Heaven with his mighty angels, In flaming fire taking
vengeance on them that know not God, and that obey not the gospel of
our Lord Jesus Christ:"* The Rapture is imminent; that is, it could
take place at any time. No signs have to be fulfilled before Jesus
comes for those of us who are saved. However, there are signs in
Matthew 24 that point to the Revelation or at least to the events
that follow seven years after the Rapture.

I find only two passages in the Bible that mention both phases
of the Second Coming in the same verse. Titus 2:13: *"Looking
for that blessed hope* (the Rapture), *and the glorious appearing* (the
Revelation) *of the great God and our Saviour Jesus Christ;"* II Timothy
4:1: *"I charge thee therefore before God, and the Lord Jesus Christ, who
shall judge the quick and the dead at his appearing* (the Rapture) *and
his kingdom* (the Revelation);"

In this message, we will notice four things concerning the Second
Advent or the Revelation of Jesus Christ.

The Warrior

Revelation 19:11: *"And I saw Heaven opened, and behold a white
horse; and he that sat upon him was called Faithful and True, and
in righteousness he doth judge and make war."* Someone may ask,
"Brother Comfort, do you think that is a real white horse?" I
absolutely think that is a real white horse. Horses were seen in
Heaven at Elijah's time.

Some may say, "Revelation 19, verse 11, does not sound like sweet baby Jesus." That is not sweet baby Jesus. When He came the first time, He came as a babe; when He comes the next time, He is coming as a warrior. Notice four names that this warrior is given.

He is called "Faithful and True." This is the **name of his sinlessness.** John 8:44 says that the devil *"is a liar, and the father of it."* Jesus is Faithful and True. Everything that Jesus is, Satan is not. Everything that Satan is, Jesus Christ is not. Several years ago, I was preaching in Singapore, and the host pastor took me into a large Buddhist complex. One building in particular had much information about the Buddhist religion. Several books on the table were available to those that visited the temple, so I picked up a book on the life of Buddha. I had a revelation as I read that book on Buddha. Buddha never claimed sinless perfection. I thought that surely Buddha would have claimed to be sinless, but he did not. I do not know of the founder of any religion who claimed sinless perfection, but Jesus Christ did. I Peter 1:18–19 says that He was a *"Lamb without blemish and without spot:"* Hebrews 4:15 says that He *"was in all points tempted like as we are, yet without sin."* I Peter 3:18 says, *"For Christ also hath once suffered for sins, the just for the unjust,..."* II Corinthians 5:21: *"For he* (God) *hath made him* (Jesus Christ) *to be sin for us, who knew no sin; that we might be made the righteousness of God in him."* He was the spotless, sinless Son of God.

My son-in-law, Mike Pelletier, worked with us in a week of evangelistic meetings preaching to the young people in the Christian school. A young man who was saved that week in the school chapels approached Mike at the end of the week and said, "Brother Mike, I have been saved this week. Up until this week, I always thought that Jesus was just a good man in the crowd that volunteered to die on the cross for the sins of the world." My son-in-law rightly responded, "Young man, if He had simply been a good man in the crowd, He could not have paid my sin debt or yours." Our Savior had to be the spotless, sinless Son of God. Pontius Pilate had to say, *"I find no fault in him."* (John 18:38) Pilate's wife said, *"Have thou nothing to do with that just man."* (Matthew 27:19) Even Judas Iscariot said, *"I have betrayed the innocent blood."* (Matthew 27:4).

When Jesus died on the cross, two thieves were crucified on either side of him. They initially railed on Jesus, but suddenly, one man had a change of mind. He said, *"We receive the due reward of our deeds: but this man hath done nothing amiss."* (Luke 23:41) A centurion stood by the cross of Christ for six hours and watched every drop of blood fall from His body to the desert sand. He heard the noise of the earthquake and saw the sun going down for three hours. He saw the rending of the veil of the temple. That centurion finally had to admit in Matthew 27:54: *"Truly this was the Son of God."*

In John 8:46, Jesus gave the Pharisees a challenge. He said, *"Which of you convinceth me of sin?"* Not a Pharisee in the crowd could say that Jesus had ever said anything that had a double meaning, nor had He ever told a half-truth. When He was facing death in John 14, Jesus said, *"…the prince of this world cometh, and hath nothing in me."* Only He could say, *"The Father hath not left me alone; for I do always those things that please him."*

Secondly, in Revelation 19, verse 12, we see **the name of His superiority.** *"He had a name written, that no man knew, but he himself."* Psalm 45:2 says, *"Thou art fairer than the children of men: grace is poured into thy lips: therefore God hath blessed thee for ever."* Psalm 89:6 says, *"For who in the Heaven can be compared unto the LORD? who among the sons of the mighty can be likened unto the LORD?"* Song of Solomon 5:16 states, *"His mouth is most sweet: yea, he is altogether lovely."* Philippians 2:9–11 says, *"Wherefore God also hath highly exalted him, and given him a name which is above* *every name: That at the name of Jesus every knee should bow, of things in Heaven, and things in earth, and things under the earth; And that every tongue should confess that Jesus Christ is Lord, to the glory of God the Father."* Certainly, Jesus alone is deserving of this name designating His superiority.

If I go into a church to preach and a lady introduces herself by the name of Joyce, right away there is a kindred spirit, because the earthly name that I love above every name is the name of my wife Joyce. However, there is a name that does something to my heartstrings that even the name of Joyce does not do, and that is the name of Jesus Christ, the most beloved name on the face of God's earth. In reading Foxe's *Book of Martyrs*, one will read about millions upon millions of people who have been willing to give their life's blood for that name which is above every name—the most beloved name on the face of God's earth. It is also the most hated name on the face of God's earth. Have you seen a carpenter trying to pound a nail, and he hits the wrong one? What does he exclaim? Does he yell, "O Mohammed!" I was watching the 2011 Masters Golf Tournament, and on the very first hole, Tiger Woods made a bad shot into the green and used God's name in vain so that everybody in the crowd around the green could hear him. I thought to myself, "Why did he not say, 'O Buddha?'" Rather, he used that name which is above every name.

My wife and I were in Puerto Rico several years ago, and I went to McDonald's early in the morning to get some breakfast food. As I was standing in line, a little girl of about eleven or twelve years of age was standing in front of me. She was speaking in the Spanish language. Suddenly, something triggered her anger, and she exclaimed so that everybody in the McDonald's could hear her, "Oh, Jesus Christ." I thought to myself, "This girl probably does not even know the English language, but she knew enough to curse that name which is above every name."

What are you going to do with Jesus? You cannot be neutral about Him. In Matthew 12:30, Jesus says, *"He that is not with me is against me; and he that gathereth not with me scattereth abroad."* Matthew 6:24 says, *"No man can serve two master."* I Corinthians 10:21 says, *"Ye cannot drink the cup of the Lord, and the cup of devils."* You cannot finish reading this sermon and be neutral about that name which is above every name. You will either receive Him or reject Him.

> What will you do with Jesus?
> Neutral you cannot be;
> Someday your heart will be asking,
> "What will He do with me?"

Thirdly, in Revelation 19, verse 13, we see **the name of His Sonship.** He *"is called The Word of God."* John 1:1–3 says, *"In the beginning was the Word, and the Word was with God, and the Word was God. The same was in the beginning with God. All things were made by him; and without him was not any thing made that was made."* John 1:14 says, *"And the Word was made flesh, and dwelt among us, (and we beheld his glory, the glory as of the only begotten of the Father,) full of grace and truth."*

Several years ago, I was in my yard on a Saturday at our home in Shelby, North Carolina, when a Jehovah's Witness engaged me in conversation. When I went upstairs after speaking with him, my wife said, "Honey, did I detect that you were talking to a Jehovah's Witness?" I said, "Yes, how did you know that?" She said, "I saw you shaking your finger at him!"

When he came up to me in my yard, I said, "Sir, do I discern that you are a Jehovah's Witness?" He said, "Yes, I am." I said, "Let me ask you a question. Does your New World translation say in John 1:1, 'In the beginning was the Word, and the Word was with God, and the Word was **a** God'?" He said, "Yes, it does." I said, "If you believe that, sir, you will die and go to Hell. I John 2:22 says, *'Who is a liar but he that denieth that Jesus is the Christ? He is antichrist,* *that denieth the Father and the Son.'"* He said, "Well, do you know what the name Jesus means?" I said, "I certainly do. It means 'I am salvation.'" He said, "No, it does not, it means, 'Jehovah is salvation.'" I said, "I am glad you said that. Look in your New World Translation at Isaiah 40:3." By the way, the best verse in the Old Testament to deal with a Jehovah's Witness regarding the deity of Christ is Isaiah 40:3 fulfilled in Luke 3:4. It says, *"The voice of him that crieth in the wilderness, Prepare ye the way of the **LORD**, make straight in the desert a highway for our God."* I said, "Now, let me ask you a few questions about this verse in Isaiah. First, what is the word L-O-R-D in capital letters?" He said, "It is the word Jehovah." I said, "You are right. Second, who does this verse prophesy?" He said, "It prophesies of John the Baptist." I said, "I am impressed. You are right. Of whom was John the Baptist the forerunner?" He said, "He was the forerunner of Jesus." I said, "I got you. Isaiah 40:3 says that he was the forerunner of Jehovah." Intelligence tells me that the Jehovah of Isaiah 40:3 is the Jesus Christ of Luke 3:4. My dear friend, unless you believe that Jesus is God of very God, you will never get to Heaven.

In Revelation 19, verse 16, we learn **the name of His Sovereignty.** He is called, *"KING OF KINGS, AND LORD OF LORDS."* Hallelujah! Revelation 11:15 says, *"And the seventh angel sounded; and there were great voices in Heaven, saying, The kingdoms of this world are become the kingdoms of our Lord, and of his Christ; and he shall reign for ever and ever."* This is the name of His Sovereignty.

In November of 1947, all of Europe was abuzz with the royal wedding of Princess Elizabeth to Phillip Mountbatten, the Duke of Edinburgh. For months, the newspapers followed the events much like they did for the recent royal wedding of Prince William and Catherine Middleton. On this day in 1947, people from all over Europe came to see the royal couple. As the procession made its way down the lanes and avenues to the chapel, the streets were filled with curious onlookers. Everyone was clamoring to see the royal couple. In the crowd that day was a young man, King Faisal II from Iraq, just twelve years old. He stood in line to see the royal couple, but something caught his eye that interested him more than the royal couple. It was the royal horses. He was a horseman, and before he realized it, he broke through the line of onlookers to get a better look at the royal horses. The police, not knowing who he was, grabbed him, shoved him back in line, rebuked him, and warned him not to break the line again. The next day, in the greatest newspaper in London, there was an apology in the headlines. "We did not know who he was!" The story went on to say that had King Faisal been wearing his crown and carrying his sceptre, the police would not have mistaken him.

One day, when Jesus Christ comes back again, the world with embarrassment will say, "We did not know who He was!" There was nothing about Jesus that resembled a King. He was born in a stinking stable and laid in a borrowed manger. He was a lowly Nazarene from Galilee. When they saw Him, there was no beauty that they should desire Him, so they put Him on a cross. When He comes the next time, the world with embarrassment will say, "We did not know who He was."

His Wardrobe

Revelation 19, verse 13 says of Jesus, *"He was clothed with a vesture dipped in blood."* What is the blood on His vesture? Some have said that it is the blood of Calvary. No! This is not Jesus coming to die on a cross. This is a warrior coming back to do battle. Isaiah 63:2–3 says, *"Wherefore art thou red in thine apparel, and thy garments like him that treadeth in the winefat? I have trodden the winepress alone; and of the people there was none with me: for I will tread them in mine anger, and trample them in my fury; and their blood shall be sprinkled upon my garments, and I will stain all my raiment."* The Bible likens it to a farmer going out into his grape arbor, trampling the grapes under, and the grape juice splattering against his garments.

> Mine eyes have seen the glory of the coming of the Lord;
> He is trampling out the vintage where the grapes of wrath
> are stored;
> He has loosed the fateful lightning of His terrible, swift sword;
> Hallelujah! My God is marching on.

At this juncture of Scripture, we have World War I. That is right. This is not World War III, but rather this is truly World War I.

From Revelation chapter sixteen, notice two things about this war. First, **the place** is designated in verse sixteen. It says, *"And he gathered them together into a place called in the Hebrew tongue Armageddon."* The word Armageddon simply means "Mount of Slaughter." This war will be fought in a triangular-shaped plot of ground east of the Mediterranean Sea and delineated between Mount Gilboa, Mount Tabor, and Mount Carmel. This 14- by 14- by 24-mile plot of ground is the most important real estate in the world. It adjoins three continents—Europe, Asia, and Africa. Anyone that controls the world by necessity will have to control that plot of ground. This place is Armageddon, the Mount of Slaughter.

Secondly, verse fourteen of Revelation chapter sixteen, identifies **the participants.** It says, *"For they are the spirits of devils, working miracles, which go forth unto the kings of the earth and of the whole world, to gather them to the battle of that great day of God Almighty."* Why did I so firmly identify this war as World War I? The world has never yet had a war when all nations were involved. This will truly be World War I! Zechariah 14:2 says that **all** nations will gather against Jerusalem. Psalm 2:2 says, *"The kings of the earth set themselves, and the rulers take counsel together, against the LORD, and against his anointed."* All nations will be involved in the War of Armageddon. If I were to ask, "What is the Battle of

Armageddon?" Most would reply that it is the last skirmish that concludes the seven-year tribulation period. There are two Greek words for the word "battle." One word means an isolated event, one battle. The second word means a series of battles or an entire war. The word for *"battle"* in Revelation 16:14 is not an isolated event; it is a series of battles or an entire war. It is my contention that the War of Armageddon includes four campaigns.

From Ezekiel chapter thirty-eight, we learn that a huge army invades from the north. Every conservative Bible scholar is in agreement that this horde that comes from the utmost north is none other than Russia. Notice Ezekiel 38:2: *"Son of man, set thy face against Gog, the land of Magog, the chief prince of Meshech and Tubal, and prophesy against him,"* In that verse, you have four proper names. First, you have Gog, a leader. Secondly, you have Magog, a land. Magog was the second grandson of Noah who migrated north to an area called Caucasus or Northern Armenia. The word Caucasus means "Gog's Fort." Russia has already identified itself as the land of Magog by sending 50,000 lead pencils to England during World War II with the inscription "Gog of Magog." Two other proper nouns are listed in verse two. Tubal has been identified as the capital city of Siberia, Tobalsk. Meshech has been identified as the city of Moscow.

When this northern army comes down to Israel, five nations will accompany them. Look at verses five and six in Ezekiel chapter thirty-eight. First of all, there is a country called Persia which, since 1935, has been known as Iran. Secondly, you have a country called Ethiopia which can be indentified from Genesis chapter two. The Garden of Eden was located in the region of Ethiopia and this encompasses the country of Iraq on today's maps. These countries are joined by Libya and by Gomer, identified as Germany, as well as Togarmah or Turkey.

When this huge army comes down, Ezekiel 39:4 says, *"Thou shalt fall upon the mountains of Israel, thou, and all thy bands, and the people that is with thee."* Millions and millions and millions of that northern horde will fall on the northern fields of Megiddo. Jeremiah 25:29 states, *"Ye shall not be unpunished: for I will call for a sword upon all the inhabitants of the earth, saith the LORD of hosts."* Isaiah 34:7 says that the time will come when *"their land shall be soaked with blood."* Verse twelve says that there will be so much carnage that it will take seven months to bury all of the dead bodies. I wonder what Israel will smell like when for seven months, millions and millions of dead bodies rot in the hot desert sun and the stench rises up to Heaven. Verse eleven states that the passengers that pass by will have to stop their noses because of the terrible stench. Ezekiel 39:9 says that it is going to take seven years to clean up all of the dead carnage and the weapons of warfare lying in the road. The first campaign is engaged by armies from the north.

Next, we must consider the armies from the south. Daniel 11:40 says, *"And at the time of the end shall the king of the south push at him (Antichrist): and the king of the north shall come against him like a whirlwind, with chariots, and with horsemen, and with many ships; and he shall enter into the countries, and shall overflow and pass over."* One of the reasons that these are coming down is because they see the emergence of this one-world dictator, the Antichrist. They are coming to wrest dominion from him. The armies from the south are the Arab and African nations.

Notice Revelation 9:13–16: *"And the sixth angel sounded, and I heard a voice from the four horns of the golden altar which is before God, Saying to the sixth angel which had the trumpet, Loose the four angels which are bound in the great river Euphrates. And the four angels were loosed, which were prepared for an hour, and a day, and a month, and a year, for to slay the third part of men. And the number of the army of the horsemen were two hundred thousand thousand* (200 million): *and I heard the number of them."* Armies are coming down from the North and up from the South, but the verses just read state that two hundred million additional soldiers are coming over from the east. Only one country in the world could field an army of two hundred million, and that is China. China, India, Japan, and Korea will come over the Euphrates River to war against Antichrist. This battle will last for a year, a month, a day, and an hour. It will slay one-third of planet earth.

As we think of world wars, consider this. In the First World War, there were eight million casualties. In the Second World War, there were seventy-eight million casualties. All of the wars of all times have produced less than two hundred million casualties. This battle at Armageddon will slay more than ten times the amount of those who have been slain in every battle in every age. Thank God this battle will not take place in our lifetime. Those of us who have accepted Christ as Savior will have been raptured to meet our Lord in the air at the time of this horrific event. The armies are coming down from the north, they are coming up from the south, and they are coming over from the east. What does that leave?

The fourth part of the armies of this great battle is identified in Revelation 13:1. *"And I stood upon the sand of the sea, and saw a beast rise up out of the sea, having seven heads and ten horns, and upon his horns ten crowns, and upon his heads the name of blasphemy."* Some may say, "There is no reason for my reading the book of the Revelation. I cannot understand it." If you have been saved for a short time, the book of the Revelation is not for you. The book of John is for you. But if you have a Bible foundation, you will find that the book of the Revelation usually interprets itself. The best commentary on Revelation 13 is Revelation 17. The Antichrist, the Beast, comes up out of the sea. Revelation 17:15 says, *"The waters which thou sawest...are peoples, and multitudes, and nations, and tongues."* As the nations are in political turmoil, out of the nations arises a satanically energized superman, the Antichrist. He has seven heads and ten horns. What are they? The Bible tells us in Revelation 17:9: *"The seven heads are seven mountains, on which the woman sitteth."* That is plain, is it not? Almost every high school student can tell you that the only city in the world that sits on seven mountains or hills is Rome. Rome will be the political capital of the world. This beast has seven heads, but he has ten horns. What are they? Revelation 17:12 tells us, *"And the ten horns which thou sawest are ten kings* (or kingdoms).*"* In the book of the Revelation, a king represents a kingdom. After the North, the South, and the East have been defeated, ten major western nations in the middle of the Tribulation period will comprise the one-world government. This one-world government will introduce to the world the one-world dictator or the Antichrist. Where is the United States of America geographically? We are in the west. What do you have religiously in the west? You have professing Christendom. It is my contention that this western group, including the United States of America, will war against the Son of God from Heaven at the end of the Tribulation period.

His Witnesses

In Revelation 19:14, it says, *"And the armies which were in Heaven followed him upon white horses, clothed in fine linen, white and clean."* Who are these armies in Heaven? If you are saved, that is you; that is me! You might ask, "How do you know this for sure?" Jesus said that it was so. In John 14:3, He says, *"that where I am, there ye may be also."* I Thessalonians 4:17 says, *"and so shall we ever be with the Lord."* Colossians 3:4 says, *"When Christ, who is our life, shall appear, then shall ye also appear with him in glory."*

We will return with our Lord on horses, and I am going to let you in on a little secret. I am not going to get on a horse until Revelation 19! That will be my next time in the saddle! My wife and three daughters love horses; and now my grandchildren love horses. I pray that they get over it. My thoughts are, "If Superman cannot handle a horse without getting a broken neck, who am I, a mortal human being who thinks that I can handle a horse?" In 1988, my wife and I were in Cody, Wyoming. I was preaching at a family ranch. Because I love my wife, I rode horses with her for four days. For the next several days, I did not want to sit down, and I did not look very good as I was walking. I do not care much how much I love my wife; I am not getting on a horse until I return with Christ in Revelation 19 as a part of the great group of spectators at the conclusion of the War of Armageddon.

His Weapon

Revelation 19:15 says, *"And out of his mouth goeth a sharp sword, that with it he should smite the nations."* I frequently hear prophetic preachers saying that God is going to destroy the world with nuclear weapons. Do not believe it! Nuclear weapons may have a part in the Tribulation, but God does not need nuclear weapons to accomplish His purpose. Did God need instruments to create the universe? No! He spoke the worlds into existence! *"Let there be light,"* and there was light.

When King Jesus comes back to Earth, Isaiah 11:4 says, *"he shall smite the earth with the rod of his mouth, and with the breath of his lips shall he slay the wicked."* All that God will need do is to say, "Let every Christ-rejecters' blood flow." Every Christ-rejecter will fall, and the bodies will be stacked on top of one another four feet deep from Dan to Beersheba, a distance of 200 miles.

Revelation 19:19–20 says, *"And I saw the beast, and the kings of the earth, and their armies, gathered together to make war against him that sat on the horse, and against his army. And the beast was taken, and with him the false prophet that wrought miracles before him, with which he deceived them that had received the mark of the beast, and them that worshipped his image. These both were cast alive into a lake of fire burning with brimstone."* The most discriminated minority is not the blacks. It is not the women. It is not the Latinos. It is Bible-believing, fundamental Christianity. The media wants to neutralize us and make us a cult. My song leader and I were in Chicago when some evil person went through the high school gunning down people with a machine gun. The media reported, "Oh, he is a fundamentalist. He is quoting Scripture."

Sometimes it seems that everything that the child of God tries to do today is defeated by the onslaughts of Satan. However, I have read the last chapter, and I know how it is going to end. One day, God Almighty will take the Antichrist and all his followers and cast them into the Lake of Fire. *"We are more than conquerors through him that loved us."*

These startling events clearly prophesied in Scripture should urge you to make ready for the coming of Christ! Just as God closed the door to the ark after years of Noah's preaching and seven additional days of grace, one day your door of opportunity for salvation will be closed. Trust Christ now for the salvation of your soul and be ready for that day when Christ returns to Earth in judgment.

My unsaved friend, are you aware that no unsaved person will enter the millennial reign of Jesus Christ? One of several things will happen if you are yet unsaved when Jesus comes:

1. You will go into the Tribulation.
2. You will not be saved in the Tribulation because you have already had your chance.
3. You may be slain in the plagues in the Tribulation.
4. Your blood may flow at one of these campaigns described in Ezekiel 39 and Revelation 9.

If you survive the Tribulation, before the Millennium there is the Judgment of the Nations in Matthew 25. Every unsaved person that survives the seven years of Tribulation will be cast into the Lake of Fire at the Judgment of the Nations.

If Jesus comes today and you are left behind, your day of grace is over.

Last Things

Chapter 5
The End of the World

Matthew 24:3: *"And as He sat upon the mount of Olives, the disciples come unto Him privately, saying, Tell us, when shall these things be? and what shall be the sign of Thy coming, and of the end of the world?"*

The word that is translated "world" in verse three is the same word that we find in the Great Commission in Matthew 28:20: *"... and, lo, I am with you alway, even unto the end of the world. Amen."* In other places in the New Testament, that same Greek word is translated as the word "age." What the disciples are asking in this verse is not, "Tell us what will be the end of this ball of fire? What will be the end of the globe?" They are asking, "Tell us what will be the end of the age?" To which age are they referring?

When approaching the study of eschatology, one must be very careful not to put the church in Matthew 24. To do so creates many difficulties in the study of last things. Everyone who erroneously believes that the church will go through either all or half of the Tribulation invariably puts the church in Matthew 24. In Matthew 24, one stands on Jewish ground; it is the Olivet Discourse. Jesus is telling His disciples all that will characterize the end of the Jewish Age.

When did the Jewish age begin? When will it end? In Daniel 9:24–25, God tells Daniel that His dealings with the Jews will last for a period of 490 years or seventy weeks. According to Daniel 9:25, this period began when the commandment was given to Nehemiah (chapter 2) to return to Jerusalem to rebuild the walls in troublous times. Thus began the seventy weeks of Daniel. God stated that from the time the commandment was given until Messiah would be cut off, exactly 483 years would expire. Any intelligent person would have to believe the validity of the Bible on the basis of this startling, fulfilled prophecy. Exactly 483 years passed from the time the commandment was given to Nehemiah to rebuild the walls until Messiah marched into Jerusalem in the triumphal entry.

We are living in a parenthetical period between the 69th and 70th week of Daniel, a period called the "church age" or the "age of the Holy Spirit." In Colossians 1:26, Paul explains that the church was an Old Testament mystery that had not been revealed, but is revealed unto us in the church age. When the Bible speaks of a mystery, it does not mean something that cannot be understood. It simply means something that has not previously been revealed. Are you aware that the Old Testament saint knew nothing about the Church Age? Imagine that!

Today God has set aside the Jews for a time. He is calling out a people for His name comprised of both saved Jews and Gentiles, and these formulate a body called the church. One day, the last person to be saved in this age of grace will complete that body. I never preach about this but what I think, "Would it not be wonderful if that last person to be saved would be saved in this service? That body would be complete, and then we would hear the shout from Heaven—the voice of the archangel—and the trump of God!"

When the church of Jesus Christ is raptured, the Antichrist will be revealed to the world. He will befriend the Jews (Daniel 9:26–27) and confirm a covenant with them for seven years. That seven-year period is the 70th Week of Daniel.

This background gives us a foundation for answering the question that the disciples gave to Jesus. Tell us, Lord Jesus, what will characterize the 70ᵗʰ Week of Daniel – or the Tribulation period? Jesus gave four answers to that question.

The Great Counterfeit

In Matthew 24:5, Jesus said, *"For many shall come in my name, saying, I am Christ; and shall deceive many."* It was not long after Jesus ascended up into Heaven until men stepped onto the scene announcing that they were the Christ. The closer that we get to the Second Coming of Jesus Christ, the more this deception will increase. If you were to go to California today, it would not take you very long to find twenty-five people who would tell you that they are the Christ. These are only shadows of that one great Antichrist that is to step on the scene.

The Jews knew that there would be a final and ultimate Antichrist. I John 2:18: *"Little children, it is the last time: and as ye have heard that antichrist shall come, even now are there many antichrists;"* How had they heard that Antichrist should come? In Genesis 3:15, God spoke to the serpent and said, *"And I will put enmity between thee and the woman, and between thy seed and her seed; it shall bruise thy head, and thou shalt bruise his heel."*

The first prophecy of Christ in the Bible is Genesis 3:15. He is the seed of the woman, not the seed of the man. He was virgin-born. Galatians 4:4–5 states, *"But when the fulness of the time was come, God sent forth his Son, made of a woman, made under the law, To redeem them that were under the law...."* On the one hand, you have the seed of the woman. On the other hand, you have the seed of the serpent. That is the first prophecy of Antichrist in the Bible. Notice that the Scripture says that the seed of the serpent would **bruise** the heel of the Messiah. When did that happen? It was fulfilled on Calvary's cross when they lapped over the feet of our Lord and pounded the ten-inch spike through the heel of the foot. However, the bruising of the heel is not a fatal wound; it is a temporary wound.

God says that the Seed of the woman would **crush** the head of the seed of the serpent. That is a fatal wound. When that first baby boy was born on planet Earth—when Eve held Cain in her arms, she thought that he was the promised Messiah. Literally in Genesis 4:1 she says, *"I have gotten THE man from the Lord."* Here is the irony. Instead of Cain being the promised Messiah, he was the first type of Antichrist in the Bible. I John 3:12: *"Not as Cain, who was of that wicked one, and slew his brother. And wherefore slew he him? Because his own works were evil, and his brother's righteous."* Cain was a type of Antichrist in that he was of Satan. He was a murderer and had the mark of a murderer put on his forehead.

Man was created on the sixth day. The number six is the number of man, and the number six in the Bible stands for failure. God rested on the seventh day. The number seven is the number of God or the number of completion and perfection. Everything God does comes up seven. Everything that man does comes up six, failure…one short of perfection. It is interesting that in the Old Testament, there are eighteen pictures of Antichrist. The number six or its combinations has to do with evil. In Satan, the false prophet, and the Antichrist, you have a triad of sixes. On the other hand, would you venture to guess how many types of Christ there are in the Old Testament? There are twenty-one. In the Father, the Son, and the Holy Spirit, you have a triad of sevens, equaling twenty-one.

The most perfect picture of Antichrist in the Bible is Judas Iscariot. I am not saying that Judas is the Antichrist, but that he is a type. A man came to me years ago and said, "Brother Comfort, I know who the Antichrist is." I said, "Oh, really! Please tell me." He said, "It is Henry Kissinger!" I said, "That's interesting." I was back in that church three years later, and he said, "Brother Comfort, when you were here before I told you that I knew who the Antichrist is, and I thought that it was Henry Kissinger. I made a mistake then, but I do know who it is now." I said, "Fine, please tell me." He said, "He runs a peanut farm in Georgia; and he is the President of the United States; and his name is Jimmy Carter." My friend, you do not know who the Antichrist is. I do not know who the Antichrist is. Furthermore, I do not care who Antichrist is. When Antichrist is revealed, I am going to be in the glory. Sadly, many people seem to be far more enamored with Antichrist than they are with Jesus Christ.

Judas is a perfect picture of Antichrist in that he is called the same name as the Antichrist: the Son of Perdition. His ministry lasted three and one-half years as that of the Antichrist. He did many miracles in the name of Christ, as the Antichrist will. He was half Jewish, as I believe that the Antichrist will be. When Judas died, he went to his own place.

I call to your attention two things about Antichrist. First of all, please note **the manner of his revealing. He is coming as an imitator of Jesus Christ.**

II Thessalonians 2:9–10: *"Even him, whose coming is after the working of Satan with all power and signs and lying wonders, And with all deceivableness of unrighteousness in them that perish; because they received not the love of the truth, that they might be saved."* During the first three and one-half years of the Tribulation period, Antichrist is coming as an imitator of Jesus Christ. Some will quibble as to whether the prefix "anti-" means *instead of* or *against*. It can mean either one. Both are true of his character. The devil is capable of doing miracles. Satan will come with all lying signs and wonders. If you are unsaved and you are left behind after the Rapture, you will believe the lie of the Antichrist. He is coming as an imitator of Jesus Christ.

Secondly, **Antichrist is coming as the opposite of Jesus Christ. He is coming as the archenemy of Jesus Christ.**

Notice the difference between Christ and Antichrist. In John 1:21, Jesus is called the Lamb of God, but in Revelation 13:1, the Antichrist is called the beast. In Daniel 11:36, the Antichrist is called the willful king, but in Revelation 19:16, Jesus is King of Kings and Lord of Lords. In II Thessalonians 2:3, the Antichrist is termed the man of sin, but in Isaiah 53:3, Jesus is called the Man of Sorrows. II Thessalonians 2:11 calls Antichrist the lie, but in John 14:6, Jesus is the Truth. Antichrist is a lawless one. Jesus Christ is the perfect one. Everything that Jesus is, Antichrist is not. Everything that Antichrist is, Jesus Christ is not. Antichrist is coming as the opposite of Jesus Christ.

The Great Confederacy

Matthew 24:6–7: *"And ye shall hear of wars and rumours of wars: see that ye be not troubled: for all these things must come to pass, but the end is not yet. For nation shall rise against nation, and kingdom against kingdom...."* At this juncture of the Tribulation period, there will not be a spot on the face of the globe where one can put his finger and say, "Here is a place where there is peace." There will be race wars, class wars, religious wars, and political wars. The entire map will be saturated in war.

Into the midst of all of this confusion comes a horde from the utmost north. Every conservative Bible scholar is in agreement that this horde from the north is none other than Russia. If you took a ruler and drew a line north of the land of Israel, inescapably you would arrive at Russia. Notice Ezekiel 38:2: *"Son of man, set thy face against Gog, the land of Magog, the chief prince of Meshech and Tubal, and prophesy against him,"* That verse includes four proper names. 1) Gog. That is a leader or a prince. 2) Magog. That is a people or a land. Magog was a grandson of Noah who migrated

north to an area called Caucasus or Northern Armenia. The word
Caucasus means, "Gog's fort." Russia has already identified
herself as being the land of Magog. In the Second World War,
Russia sent 50,000 lead pencils to England, and on those pencils
was the inscription "Gog of Magog."

Continuing with the other proper names listed in Ezekiel 38:2, 3)
Meshech. That has been identified as being the city of Moscow.
4) Tubal. That has been identified as the capital city of Siberia,
Tobolsk.

When Russia comes down (they are coming on horseback, the
only way that they could inconspicuously get into the land), five
nations will accompany them. Ezekiel 38:5–6: *"Persia, Ethiopia,
and Libya with them; all of them with shield and helmet: Gomer, and
all his bands; the house of Togarmah of the north quarters, and all his
bands: and many people with thee."* First of all, there is a country
called Persia. What is Persia today? Iran. In 1935, the name Persia
was changed to Iran. Secondly, there is a country called Ethiopia.
Thirdly, there is a country called Libya. Fourthly, there is a country
called Gomer. These people have been identified as a people of
Germany. It used to be popular to preach that Gomer was East
Germany. Ezekiel did not say that it was East Germany. *"Gomer,
and all his bands."* Ezekiel looked into the future and saw a time
when the Berlin Wall would be torn down. There would be no
more two Germanys, but there would be one Germany and all
of Germany will be sympathetic with that Northern invasion.
Already there have been public demonstrations in Germany
against Israel. The scene is being set for all nations to turn their
backs on the nation of Israel. Fifthly, there is a country called
Togarmah. These people have been identified as the people of
Turkey.

Consider three important things regarding this invasion. First of
all, note **the time of the invasion**. Ezekiel 38:8 says that it happens

when Israel is dwelling safely in the land. In verse sixteen of that same chapter, we learn that the invasion occurs when they are dwelling safely in a land of unwalled villages. This is partly true today. When Ezekiel made that prophecy, he put his neck on the chopping block. The statement in those days was "A city that had no walls was no city at all." What was the import of that saying? Walls were a matter of protection. If a city did not have any walls, it would be only a matter of time until the people would be exterminated. Ezekiel looked out in the future and knew that one day Israel would be dwelling without walls. That is true today. Is Israel dwelling in peace in their land? Obviously not! When will they be dwelling in peace? Daniel 9:26–27 has the answer. When the Antichrist befriends the Jews and confirms a covenant with them for seven years at some point near the outset of the Tribulation, then the Jews will be dwelling in their land of unwalled villages in peace. Thus, the invasion of the northern horde could not happen in the second half of the tribulation period, because in the middle of the Tribulation period, the Antichrist will turn against the Jew. This invasion will also not happen before the rapture. It will happen at some point in the first three and one-half years of the Tribulation.

Secondly, notice **the reasons for the invasion**. Why are Russia and her hordes coming down?

The first words of verse 12 and the last words of verse 13 in Ezekiel chapter 38 give us the reason for the invasion. They are coming down **to take a spoil.** Perhaps you are aware that the land of Israel has been called "the Jewel-Box of the World." In the 1960's, the minerals in the Dead Sea were evaluated at 1 trillion, 270 billion dollars—equivalent to more than the wealth of the rest of the world at that time. It has been estimated that there are 45 million tons of unprocessed chemicals in the Dead Sea, including a rich reserve of oil. It has been said that the minerals in the basin of the Dead Sea are worth more than the gold that has been dug from the bowels of the earth in 6,000 years of human history. Is it any wonder then that the northern horde is coming down to take a spoil?

You will also notice in the last few words of Ezekiel 38:12 that Israel dwells *"in the midst of the land."* In the margin of my Bible, the word "navel" is given as an additional explanation for the word "midst." In other words, Israel is the navel of the earth. That small country joins three continents: Europe, Asia, and Africa. Whoever it is that seeks to control the world must of necessity control this plot of ground from Dan to Beersheba. The northern horde will come down because of **the geographic significance of the land.**

Ezekiel 38:16 states that God is going to permit it all to happen so that **He will be magnified in the eyes of the nations.** Ezekiel 38:16b: *"...that the heathen may know me, when I shall be sanctified in thee, O Gog, before their eyes."* Ezekiel 38:23: *"Thus will I magnify myself, and sanctify myself; and I will be known in the eyes of many nations, and they shall know that I am the LORD."* Ezekiel 39:22: *"So the house of Israel shall know that I am the LORD their God from that day and forward."*

Because of what Jesus does on their behalf in this northern invasion, Zechariah 12:10 says of the Jews, *"...and they shall look upon me whom they have pierced."* They will claim Him as their Messiah, and a nation will be born again as in a day. Romans 11:26–27 says, *"And so all Israel shall be saved:"* because of what Jesus does in that northern invasion. Through Israel's conversion (Revelation 7:9–17), 144,000 Jewish evangelists will take the gospel of the kingdom throughout the world, and through their preaching, a multitude of Gentiles that no man could number will be saved.

Give attention now to **the results of the invasion.**

Ezekiel 39:4: *"Thou shalt fall upon the mountains of Israel, thou, and all thy bands, and the people that is with thee...."* Millions and millions and millions of that northern horde will fall in the northern fields of Megiddo. Ezekiel 39:12 says that it will take seven months to bury all of the dead bodies. I wonder what Israel will smell like when for seven months, millions and millions of dead bodies are stacked on top of one another rotting in the intense heat of the desert sun. Ezekiel 39:11 says that when the passengers travel by, they will have to stop their noses because of the terrible stench. Ezekiel 39:9 affirms that it will take seven years to clean up all of the dead carnage and the weapons of warfare lying in the road. What will God do to that northern horde? Ezekiel 39:9 says that He will send fire to devour all those that have remained in Russia and the isles that surround Russia and all the weapons that remain.

However, that recourse does not take care of Israel's chief antagonist.

The Great Conflict

Matthew 24:9: *"Then shall they deliver you (the Jews) up to be afflicted, and shall kill you: and ye shall be hated of all nations for my name's sake."* Certainly, one can see this coming to pass.

The conflict is twofold. First of all it is **Antichrist against the Jew.** Daniel 7:21 says that Antichrist makes war with the saints of God and prevails against them. Daniel 7:25 says that he *"shall wear out the saints of the most High...."* Daniel 8:24 says that he *"shall destroy the mighty and the holy people."*

In Revelation 12, a woman gives birth to a man-child. The woman pictures Israel. The man-child was Jesus Christ. The Bible says that after the man-child was born, the dragon (or Satan) tried to devour the man-child. This took place in the days of Herod the king. If Herod had exterminated every baby two years of age and under, he would have done away with the man-child; but God did not allow that to happen. Instead Satan turned against the woman—the Jew that produced the man-child.

The Bible says that God will bring the Jew into the wilderness to a place called Sela (Isaiah 16:1) which is the Rose City of Petra. It is an exciting thing to go to Petra. One can only enter Petra today through a narrow canyon; most people make the trek on horseback. As you look up into the high stone walls of the city, you see thousands of holes in the caves. There are Bibles hidden in the caves of Petra, because the Jews are one day going to flee there, and someone is going to feed them there for three and one-half years. Who do you think will feed these Jewish refugees? I would like to think that perhaps it will be the United States of America. Unfortunately though, I believe that one day, for political expediency, our country will figuratively stick a knife in the back of the Jew. By the way, you cannot be right with God and be anti-Semitic. If you get conservative literature in the mail that is anti-Semitic, throw it in the garbage can.

Secondly, **Antichrist is against God Himself.** Matthew 24:15 says, *"When ye therefore shall see the abomination of desolation, spoken of by Daniel the prophet, stand in the holy place...."* What is the meaning of the terminology, *"the abomination of desolation"*? Do you know that there were 400 silent years between the Old Testament and the beginning of the New Testament—400 years when God did not communicate Scripture to man? During that time period, Antiochus Epiphanes, to show his hatred for God and the Jews, went into the Jew's holy place, erected an image of the god Zeus, and demanded that everyone fall down and worship the image of that false god. He also desecrated the Jews' holy place by offering swine, an unclean animal, as a sacrifice.

In the middle of the Tribulation period, when the covenant is broken with the Jew, Antichrist will go into the Jews' holy place and erect an image of himself. (By the way, the Jews are looking forward to a rebuilt Temple.) Everyone will be forced to fall down before that image or before the Antichrist himself and receive his mark in their forehead or in their hand. Already, the United States government is working on a Personal Identification Number no larger than the head of a hypodermic needle that will one day be deposited under the skin of every American citizen. One day, that identification system will be worldwide. Things are happening faster than one can imagine! However, it will all end right!

The Great Climax

Matthew 24:30 says, *"And then shall appear the sign of the Son of man in Heaven: and then shall all the tribes of the earth mourn, and they shall see the Son of man coming in the clouds of Heaven with power and great glory."* Thus, we see the glorious conclusion!

The conflict of the ages began in Isaiah 14:12–15. A created being named Lucifer (his name means "light-bearer") was the most beautiful of God's creation, but he was not satisfied just with beauty. Five times in three verses, Lucifer said, "I will...I will...I will." Finally, he said, *"I will be like the most High."* That statement was the beginning of the conflict of the ages. Ever since that time, it has been Satan against God. It has been Antichrist against Jesus Christ. It has been evil against good. Notice several things about the culmination of this conflict.

First of all, take note of **the place**. Revelation 16:16 says, *"And he gathered them together into a place called in the Hebrew tongue Armageddon."* I have made note in the margin of my Bible that "Armageddon" is the "Mount of Slaughter." This is the place where the conflict of the ages will be decided. Geographically, this battle will be fought in the place that Napoleon Bonaparte identified as "the most perfect battlefield in the world." It is a triangular plot of ground with Mount Tabor, Mount Carmel, and Mount Gilboa as the vertices. This is truly the place of World War number one!

Secondly, note **the participants**. Revelation 16:14 says, *"For they are the spirits of devils, working miracles, which go forth unto the kings of the earth and of the whole world, to gather them to the battle of that great day of God Almighty."* Why did I say that it would be World War number one being fought in that perfect battlefield? Truly, there has never before been a war when all nations of the world were involved. If I were to ask knowledgeable laymen versed in the Scriptures to define and describe the Battle of Armageddon, I would likely get this answer. "It is that last skirmish at the end of the seven years that completes the Tribulation." The Greek language has two words that can be used for the word "battle." One word means "one isolated event or skirmish." The second word means "a series of battles or an entire war." The word used in Revelation 16:14 is not the word for one isolated event, but rather it denotes a series of battles or an entire war.

I believe that the War of Armageddon really contains four campaigns. First of all, in Ezekiel 38 and 39, Russia will be coming down. Secondly, in Daniel 11:40, the kings of the south, the Arab and the African nations, will join. Then in Revelation 9:13–21, 200 million Asians led by the kings of the east come over the Euphrates River. You have the north, the south, and the east. What does that leave? That leaves ten major western nations.

Revelation 13:1 speaks of the beast with seven heads and ten horns. The ten horns are ten kings or kingdoms. At the middle of the Tribulation period, you have the revived Roman Empire—ten major western nations who will comprise the world government in the middle of the Tribulation period. Where is the United States of America geographically? We are in the west. One of two things will be true at this juncture. Either the United States of America will be one of those ten major western nations, or it could be that we have so morally perverted ourselves from within that at this time of the Tribulation, we will no longer be a world power. Regardless of whether we are one of the ten major nations or whether we are a subservient nation, religiously the western nations represent professing Christianity. Very succinctly, the last battle of the War of Armageddon will be a war between professing Christianity and the very Son of God from Heaven. Think of it. The United States of America will war against the Son of God from Heaven at the conclusion of the Tribulation period.

How will all this end? I draw your attention to Zephaniah 3:8, a verse with significant prophetic meaning. What is the significance of that verse? A portion of the verse reads, *"...for all the earth shall be devoured with the fire of my jealousy."* Only one verse in the Old Testament contains every Hebrew letter of the Hebrew alphabet, and that verse is Zephaniah 3:8. The Jewish scribe took that to mean that the entire purpose of the planet Earth is fulfilled in Zephaniah 3:8.

One day, God Almighty will take the Antichrist and cast him into the Lake of Fire. However, *"We are more than conquerors through him that loved us"* (Romans 8:37).

Revelation 19:17–18 says, *"And I saw an angel standing in the sun; and he cried with a loud voice, saying to all the fowls that fly in the midst of Heaven, Come and gather yourselves together unto the supper of the great God; That ye may eat the flesh of kings, and the flesh of captains, and the flesh of mighty men, and the flesh of horses, and of them that sit on them, and the flesh of all men, both free and bond, both small and great."* Five times in those two verses, the word "flesh" is used. Flesh, flesh, flesh, flesh, flesh. The bottom line is this. If you go into the Tribulation period and you are not slain by the plagues in the Tribulation period, then your blood will flow at the Great Supper of God Almighty.

You have a choice of suppers. In Luke 14, there is the Invitation Supper of Salvation. You are a sinner. Jesus Christ died on Calvary paying the penalty for your sins to keep you from an eternal Hell. God says that the door is open. Will you accept the invitation to salvation?

If you refuse that supper and you go into the Tribulation period, your blood may flow at the Great Supper of God Almighty in God's final judgment on this earth. Which supper do you choose to attend?

Last Things

Chapter 6
History's Greatest Imitator

Some have said, "Why should I bother reading the Book of the Revelation, because I cannot understand it?" If you have only been saved for a short time, then the book of the Revelation is not for you. The book of John is for you. If you have been saved for awhile, you will find that the Book of Revelation generally interprets itself.

As far as I can tell, only one book in the Bible promises a blessing to its readers and its hearers. That is the book of the Revelation. Notice Revelation 1:3, which says, *"Blessed is he that readeth, and they that hear the words of this prophecy, and keep those things which are written therein: for the time is at hand."* It says blessed are they that read it. It does not say one thing about understanding it, does it? If you read the Book of Revelation, God promises you a blessing. He says blessed are they that hear it. If you listen to the preaching of a message from the Book of Revelation, God promises you a blessing. However, if you go to sleep during the preaching of that message, you will not get a blessing, and you may get a hymnal upside your head!

In order to understand the book, there is a key that unlocks the door. That key is Revelation 1:19: *"Write the things which thou hast seen, and the things which are, and the things which shall be hereafter."* God gives a simple three-fold outline to bear in mind as you come to the Book of the Revelation.

1. He said, *"Write the things which thou hast seen"*—**the things of the past tense.** Revelation 1:9–20 is the vision that John had

of Jesus Christ while on the isle of Patmos. By the way, if you want to find out what Jesus looked like, you will not do so by looking at a portrait that someone has painted. I am amused at people that have visions of Jesus. When you ask them what Jesus looked like in their vision, they invariably point to a picture of Jesus displayed on the wall of the church building. They will say, "He looked just like that picture over there." My question is, "With what camera was that picture taken?" Incidentally, most visions are caused from eating too much before going to bed at night. If you want a recipe for a vision, prepare an onion sandwich, sprinkle it liberally with Tabasco sauce, and enjoy it just before bedtime while drinking a glass of buttermilk. You will definitely have a vision. If you want to find out what Jesus looked like, go to Revelation 1:9–20.

2. *"Write the things...which are"*—**the things of the present tense.** In Revelation chapters two and three, God writes to seven churches of Asia Minor. Were there only seven churches in that region? No, there were many. The number seven is the number of completion or perfection. In these seven churches, we have a Bible panorama of the church from its inception until the time that Jesus Christ raptures us. It is interesting to notice in Revelation 2:1 that Jesus is in the **midst** of the churches. In Revelation 3:14–22, the Laodicean Age, Jesus is no longer in the midst of the churches, but rather He is **on the outside.** I believe that the National Council of Churches and the World Council of Churches have put Him on the outside. Their attitude is, "Jesus, we do not need You or the Bible. We have plenty of money in our coffers. We have large buildings. We do not need You."

The Bible paints a bleak picture of the Laodicean Age. However, there is a ray of sunshine that breaks through. In Revelation 3:20, Jesus says, *"Behold, I stand at the door, and knock: if any man hear my voice, and open the door, I will come in*

to him, and will sup with him, and he with me." The invitation is
"...if any man." Revelation 22:17 says, *"And the Spirit and the
bride say, Come. And let him that heareth say, Come. And let him
that is athirst come. And whosoever will, let him take the water
of life freely."* That invitation is the ray of sunshine in this
Laodicean Age.

3. From Revelation chapters four through twenty-two, we see
   the third part of the outline for the Book of the Revelation:
   "Write...the things which shall be hereafter"—**the things of
   the future tense.** Some may say, "Brother Comfort, will the
   church go through the Tribulation?" There is **a** church that
   will go through the Tribulation. That is the Bride of Antichrist,
   the ecumenical church. In Revelation 17:1, she is called
   "the great whore that sitteth upon many waters." In Revelation
   17:5, she is called *"MYSTERY, BABYLON THE GREAT, THE
   MOTHER OF HARLOTS AND ABOMINATIONS OF THE
   EARTH."* God has an admonition for any saved person who
   is a part of a church that supports the National Council of
   Churches or the World Council of Churches, the ecumenical
   church. In Revelation 18:4, He says, *"Come out of her, my
   people, that ye be not partakers of her sins, and that ye receive not of
   her plagues."*

On the other hand, those of us who are saved will not go
through the Tribulation. If I had only this simple three-point
outline for the book of the Revelation, it is enough to tell
me that those of us who are saved will not go through the
Tribulation. From Revelation 6 through Revelation 19, the
judgments of God are being poured out upon the earth.
Believers are not on Earth during Revelation 6–19; we are
viewed from a Heavenly viewpoint. It is my contention that
the Rapture takes place in Revelation chapter four, verses one
through three.

Notice Revelation 4:1–3: *"After this I looked, and, behold, a door was opened in Heaven: and the first voice which I heard was as it were of a trumpet talking with me; which said, Come up hither, and I will shew thee things which must be hereafter. And immediately I was in the spirit: and, behold, a throne was set in Heaven, and one sat on the throne. And he that sat was to look upon like a jasper and a sardine stone: and there was a rainbow round about the throne, in sight like unto an emerald."* John sees a Door. Who is that Door? According to Scripture, Jesus Christ is the Door. In John 10:9, He said, "I am the door: by me if any man enter in, he shall be saved, and shall go in and out, and find pasture." John looks up, sees the Door, and hears the voice of the trumpet. Recall the words of I Thessalonians 4:16 and I Corinthians 15:51. Our Lord is coming with the trump of God.

John sees the Door, hears the trump, and (I like the second word of verse two!), *"Immediately I was in the spirit."* He was not left behind to go through the Tribulation, but the moment he saw the Door and heard the trump, he was immediately standing before the Throne of God.

Our text passage, Revelation 6:1–2, reads,

"And I saw when the Lamb opened one of the seals, and I heard, as it were the noise of thunder, one of the four beasts saying, Come and see.
And I saw, and behold a white horse: and he that sat on him had a bow; and a crown was given unto him: and he went forth conquering, and to conquer."

Whenever you see horses in the Bible as being symbolic, they are generally symbolic of judgment or warfare. After the church of Jesus Christ is raptured, there will be judgment and warfare. The oriental or eastern person looked upon the horse with awe, reverence, and fear. To them, this beast represented march, attack, and battle. In an ancient military parade, the victor always led the procession by riding a white horse.

Generally, in the Bible, white is symbolic of the holiness of God or the righteousness of Jesus Christ. Revelation 4:4 says, "*...I saw four and twenty elders sitting, clothed in white raiment; and they had on their heads crowns of gold.*" Because white is generally symbolic of the holiness of God, some people mistakenly say, "This must be Jesus on the white horse." There are three reasons why I do not believe that the rider on this horse is Jesus Christ.

1. Who was it that opened the seal? It was the Lamb. Who is the Lamb? John the Baptist identified the Lamb. In John 1:29 and John 1:36, he pointed to Jesus and said, "*Behold the Lamb of God, which taketh away the sin of the world.*" Logically, if the Lamb opens the seal, the Lamb is not going to be on the white charger.

2. The Bible says that this rider has a bow; he has a weapon in his hand. When King Jesus comes back to earth, He will need no weapon. Isaiah 11:4 says, "*...he shall smite the earth with the rod of his mouth, and with the breath of his lips shall he slay the wicked.*" This rider has a weapon; Jesus will need no weapon.

3. Unto this rider is given a crown. There are two Greek words in the New Testament for crown. One word is always associated with humanity. It is the word we get from the stoning of Stephen, a "*stephanos*" crown. The second word is the word *diadem*. That word is associated with deity. Revelation 19:12 tells us that right now on the head of Jesus are many diadems. The rider in Revelation 6 wears the crown connected with humanity, not the crown connected with deity. You may say, "If this is not Jesus Christ, then who is he?" This is the one who is coming instead of Christ or against Christ. The Bible calls him, Antichrist. I call him "History's Greatest Imitator."

As far as I can tell, there is only one writer in the Bible to use the term antichrist. It is the same one who wrote the book of the

Revelation, the apostle John. I find it four times in John's writings: I John 2:18, I John 2:22, I John 4:2–3, and II John 7.

The book of II Thessalonians was written to deal with a problem concerning the Antichrist. According to Acts 17, Paul spent three weeks at Thessalonica. During those three weeks, he taught the Thessalonian Christians about many things, and evidently one of his topics was a study of last things. After his departure from them, someone then wrote to the church in Thessalonica and told them that the persecution they were experiencing was the beginning of the Day of the Lord or the Tribulation period. To top it all off, that writer forged Paul's name on the end of the letter. Supposedly, this letter from the apostle Paul stated that the Christians were going through the Tribulation. This was quite disturbing to the believers, so Paul wrote a letter to correct the error.

II Thessalonians 2:1–2 says, *"Now we beseech you, brethren, by the coming of our Lord Jesus Christ, and by our gathering together unto him, That ye be not soon shaken in mind, or be troubled, neither by spirit, nor by word, nor by letter as from us, as that the day of Christ is at hand."* Do you see what Paul is saying? He is cautioning the believers: "Listen, if someone sends you a letter and tells you that you are going through the Tribulation, do not believe it. Even if my name is signed at the end of that letter, do not believe it." Why? There are two things that must take place before the Tribulation begins. II Thessalonians 2:3 says, *"Let no man deceive you by any means: for that day (or the Tribulation) shall not come, except*

1. *there come a falling away first, and*
2. *that man of sin be revealed, the son of perdition."*

First of all, there has to be a falling away. In the Greek language, there is a definite article before the phrase "falling away"—**the** falling away. What does that article indicate? It is a falling away about which he had previously spoken to them. Verse five says,

"Remember ye not, that, when I was yet with you, I told you these things?" To what great falling away previously mentioned is he referring? The only other book that we know that Paul wrote to the Thessalonians was I Thessalonians, and in those five chapters you do not read one word about an apostasy, a falling away from the truth.

The phrase "falling away" can also be translated as "a departure." Before the day marking the beginning of the Tribulation comes, there has to be **the great departure**. I Thessalonians 4:16–17 describes it: *"For the Lord himself shall descend from Heaven with a shout, with the voice of the archangel, and with the trump of God: and the dead in Christ shall rise first: Then we which are alive and remain shall be caught up together with them in the clouds, to meet the Lord in the air: and so shall we ever be with the Lord."* This is one of the best proof texts in the Bible that those of us who are saved will not go through the Tribulation. Before that day comes, there has to be the Great Departure, the Rapture of the church.

Secondly, **that man of sin must be revealed.** According to Daniel 9:26–27, when the Antichrist is revealed to the world, he befriends the Jewish nation, and confirms a covenant with the Jews for seven years. For many years, I preached that the event that triggered the beginning of the Tribulation was the Rapture. However, many years ago, a layman in Ohio pointed out to me that my theory was not true. The event that officially begins Tribulation is when the Antichrist confirms the covenant with the Jews. How long will the covenant last? It will last for seven years. How long will the Tribulation last? It will last for seven years. The moment that the Antichrist confirms the covenant, the Seventieth Week of Daniel or the seven-year Tribulation period has begun.

Notice three observations regarding the impending arrival of the Antichrist.

The Moment of His Appearing

II Thessalonians 2:6–8 reads,

> *"And now ye know what withholdeth that he might be revealed in his time.*
> *For the mystery of iniquity doth already work: only he who now letteth will let, until he be taken out of the way.*
> *And then shall that Wicked be revealed, whom the Lord shall consume with the spirit of his mouth, and shall destroy with the brightness of his coming."*

In this passage, we read two "he's," and they are in contrast. The first "he" in verse six refers to the Antichrist.

The "he" in verse seven refers to the Holy Spirit, *"...he who now letteth will let."* The Old English word "letteth" means "restrains" or "hinders." He will restrain or hinder until he be taken out of the way. Restraint or conviction in the heart is the work of the Holy Spirit. We do not preach as do the Charismatics and other groups that the indwelling of the Holy Spirit is an experience that occurs at some point other than at salvation. The moment you receive Christ as Savior, God the Holy Spirit makes His residence in your body. I Corinthians 3:16 says, *"Know ye not that ye are the temple of God, and that the Spirit of God dwelleth in you?"* II Corinthians 6:16 states, *"And what agreement hath the temple of God with idols? for ye are the temple of the living God."*

An unsaved man may curse his wife many times when she is getting ready to go to church, but if he has half a brain, he ought to get down on his knees and thank God for her. He should beg God to keep that Christian wife around awhile longer, because when God raptures that saved wife, all hell is going to break loose on this earth. On your job, you may be called a "Funny-mentalist." You may be called a "fun-damn-mentalist." But those unsaved friends should be thankful for you, because the only thing keeping the judgment of God from taking place is the presence of every child of God. Once we are raptured, the Restrainer is gone.

This truth is tremendously illustrated by the nation of Israel in II Chronicles chapter fifteen, when there came a time that the restraints of the judgment of God were gone. II Chronicles 15:3 says, *"Now for a long season Israel hath been without the true God, and without a teaching priest, and without law."* The true God, the teaching priest, and the law were the three restrainers holding back the judgment of God.

When the church of Jesus Christ is raptured, the world will be without the true God. The Holy Spirit who lives in the body of the believer will no longer serve in His present relationship to the world. Secondly, the teaching priests will be missing. God's prophets are all raptured. Thirdly, mankind will be without the Law. I do not speak of civil authority, but of the Word of God.

People ask me frequently what I think of Rick Warren. My stock answer is this. "Rick Warren does not have a Bible." What do I mean? Rick Warren believes in thought inspiration, dynamic equivalency. He does not believe in word inspiration, which is also termed "formal equivalency." Ambassador Baptist College does not believe in thought inspiration. I do not believe in thought inspiration! If you believe that God inspired only the thoughts of the men who penned the Bible, you can make the Bible say anything you want it to say. When I was in college, we called that neo-orthodoxy: the belief that the Bible is not the Word of God but that it contains the Word of God. From all that I have read of Rick Warren, that is his belief.

Most of the versions that come off the presses now are prepared by those who believe in thought inspiration. Some have said, "I want a Bible that reads like a newspaper." There is no power in the newspaper, but there is power in the Bible! In fifty years of ministry, I have preached over 1,400 crusades, and there has not been one crusade in all of those fifty years that someone's life had not been transformed by the power of God's Word. It still works!

So what was the result of Israel being without those three restraints? II Chronicles 15:5–6 says, *"And in those times there was no peace to him that went out, nor to him that came in, but great vexations were upon all the inhabitants of the countries. And nation was destroyed of nation, and city of city: for God did vex them with all adversity."* Do you see the picture? When the restrainers were gone, the judgment of God took place. When the church of Jesus Christ is raptured, the restrainers will be gone and the judgment of God will take place. Does that sound strangely like Matthew 24:21–22? *"For then shall be great tribulation, such as was not since the beginning of the world to this time, no, nor ever shall be. And except those days should be shortened, there should no flesh be saved: but for the elect's sake those days shall be shortened."*

It is my contention that at this point, World War One begins. This is no mistake. I purposely refer to The Battle of Armageddon as World War One, for it truly is the first war in which the entire earth will be engaged. This war is described in Ezekiel chapter 38 and Revelation chapter nineteen, as well as in other chapters in this book.

The Manner of His Appearing

II Thessalonians 2:9–10, speaking of the Antichrist, says, *"Even him, whose coming is after the working of Satan with all power and signs and lying wonders, And with all deceivableness of unrighteousness in them that perish; because they received not the love of the truth, that they might be saved."* The manner of his appearing is that he is coming with all lying signs and wonders. The closer that we get to the Second Coming of Christ to Earth, the more the occult and spiritism will be prevalent. The average Christian is not aware that the devil is capable of doing miracles. In Luke 9:1, Jesus sent out twelve disciples to do all manner of miracles, and you will recall that one of those disciples was Judas Iscariot. Judas' ministry was not in any way inferior to the other eleven disciples. Satan is capable of doing miracles.

Let me paint for you a hypothetical situation. What if my long-time song leader, Brother Brubaker, in one of his animated three-foot jumps, comes down on the platform and suddenly has a massive coronary and drops over dead? I get down on my hands and knees, and I feel his pulse and say, "Folks, there is nothing there." I listen to his heartbeat, and I say, "Folks, there is nothing there." I examine his head and I say, "There is nothing there—inside or out!" Suddenly, a physician rushes to the platform and offers to examine Brother Brubaker. He examines him from head to toe and then speaks to the congregation. "Ladies and Gentlemen, this is a sad night. If we had the capability to medevac Larry Brubaker to the finest hospital in Charlotte in five minutes, it would be of no benefit. Larry Brubaker is dead." Then I step up once again and say, "Doctor, please step back." I lean over and with authority say, "Larry Brubaker, in the name of Jesus Christ, stand to your feet!" Suddenly, Brother Brubaker leaps up and takes up his energetic song leading once again. Would that "miracle" prove that I was of God? Absolutely not! Satan is capable of doing miracles. Some healers say, "If you want a feeling, put your hand on the radio." I can tell you a better way to get a feeling. Put your hand **in** the radio, and you will really have a great feeling.

Antichrist is coming with all lying signs and wonders. The fastest growing religion in America, contrary to what you may think, is not Islam, but Wicca. Wicca has grown by one thousand percent in the last ten years. A man in South Bend, Indiana, gave a sad testimony. He said, "Brother Comfort, I innocently got mixed up with a Satan-worshipping crowd. I thought I could win them to Christ, but it was the greatest mistake that I ever made in my life. I even went to the extent of attending their black masses. I saw things that have scarred my mind and keep me awake at night." You would be amazed at the amount of young people that have gravitated to the Satan worshipping movement, and many of them begin that journey through a simple, Ouija board. If you have in your possession demonic role-playing games or Ouija board, you are playing with Satanism. Get those things out of your house! Here is another grave warning. Any young person who feeds on MTV or the rock-video channels is also leaving the door open for demon possession or demon obsession.

A lady in Illinois told me her experience with the Ouija board. She said, "Brother Comfort, when I was young, I played with the Ouija board frequently. Nobody ever warned me about it. One night in the youth group, my youth pastor warned me about the danger of the game. I was offended and confronted him saying, 'You have offended me by your teaching against the Ouija board. I play with it frequently and see nothing wrong or dangerous about it.'" The youth pastor said, "Let me give you a challenge. When you get home this evening, take out your Ouija board, and ask it this question: 'Ouija board, who is your master?' I guarantee that it will spell out devil." The woman said, "I will disprove that." She went home, took out her Ouija board and asked, "Ouija board, who is your master?" The Ouija board began to spell out "S-A-." She said, "I knew that it would not spell the word devil." However, it spelled S-A-T-A-N.

Another lady in Portland, Oregon, asked to tell me about her family's experience. She said, "Brother Comfort, our family played with the Ouija board frequently. Everybody in the family was saved except for my husband. One Sunday in our evening church service, our pastor warned us about the Ouija board. He said,

'You do not get rid of the Ouija board by putting it on the shelf in the closet. You throw it in the garbage can or you burn it. You have to get it out of your house.'" (By the way, you also do not get rid of rock music by putting it on the shelf in your closet. Many times before these rock performers will record their music, they ask the blessings of Satan upon that music. A Satanic oppression or depression is often connected with that music. Get it out of your house all together!) That night the woman went home from church and told her unsaved husband about the pastor's sermon. She said, "Honey, the pastor said that we need to throw the Ouija board in the fireplace. With your permission, I would like to throw the Ouija board in the fireplace and get it out of our house." He said, "Fine with me! You have my permission." The whole family gathered around the fireplace as they threw the Ouija board in the fire. She said, "Brother Comfort, you cannot imagine the screams and cries that emanated from that Ouija board." The blessing of that story is that in a very short time, the husband of that family came to know Christ as Savior. He had witnessed the power and reality of Satan and knew that He needed Christ!

I have been asked, "Brother Comfort, have you heard about the Roman Catholic Church in Virginia in which the statue of Mary is reported to be weeping? Do you believe it could really happen?" I said, "Of course, I believe that could happen." The devil is capable of doing miracles.

The Message of His Appearing

I Thessalonians 5:2–4: *"For yourselves know perfectly that the day of the Lord so cometh as a thief in the night. For when they shall say, Peace and safety; then sudden destruction cometh upon them, as travail upon a woman with child; and they shall not escape. But ye, brethren, are not in darkness, that that day should overtake you as a thief."*

117

Thank God that the day of Antichrist's appearing will not overtake us as a thief. We are not children of the night, but children of the day. He will overtake the world as a thief in the night, but he will not overtake the child of God.

Have you ever noticed the analogy that God makes concerning the Tribulation? He compares it to a woman travailing in the pain of childbirth. All mothers remember the night that the labor pains started. They start out slowly. In fact, there is sometimes the possibility of a bit of sleep between contractions. But then those pains intensify and intensify until just before that baby is born, the woman thinks it is impossible to remain sane and experience that type of pain! Can you imagine a woman being in labor pains for seven years with the pains never ceasing? The pain keeps increasing and intensifying! That is the way God describes the Tribulation period.

Notice Antichrist's message. *"For when they shall say, Peace...."* Compare that message with the message of Jesus when He was on earth. Just before He ascended up into Heaven, He said in John 14:27: *"Peace I leave with you, my peace I give unto you: not as the world giveth, give I unto you."* John 16:33 says, *"These things I have spoken unto you, that in me ye might have peace."* Jesus Christ offered mankind an internal peace that would come by receiving Him as Lord and Savior. The Antichrist knows nothing about internal peace, so his message will totally be an external peace. A person cannot be at peace with his neighbor, nor can nation be at peace with nation, until first of all they are at peace with God.

If you and I were to visit the Wailing Wall in Old Jerusalem at any time of the day or night, we would see Jews facing that wall, rocking back and forth, and chanting. In the tiny holes in the wall where the rocks have eroded or do not fit tightly together, we would find hundreds, perhaps thousands, of tiny pieces of paper rolled up and stuffed into the crevices. On nearly every one of those papers is penned one of three prayer requests.

1. Pray for the soon coming of our Messiah. In many places around Israel, one can see signs that say "Pray for the coming of the Messiah."

2. Pray that our persecutions will be over. Jerusalem has been leveled to the ground eighteen times, more than any other city around the world. It is an indestructible city.

3. Pray for the soon rebuilding of our temple.

If you have ever attended a Jewish wedding, you likely observed that at the conclusion of the ceremony, the groom took a glass and crushed it under his heel. Why did he do that? That ritual is to commemorate the destruction of the temple in 70 AD when Titus and his Roman soldiers marched into Jerusalem and leveled the city. From that time until this, the Jews have been without a blood sacrifice because they have no temple. In May of 2010, I had the privilege to travel in the Bible Lands. At the Temple Institutes, the guide showed us the replica of the rebuilt temple. Plans are already drawn to rebuild the temple. In fact, the majority of the furniture is already made for the temple, but they have no temple in which to place it. She stated, "We believe that God is going to place this temple on the temple mount. We believe that God will miraculously remove what is already there so that we can rebuild our temple." When the Antichrist is revealed to the world and befriends the Jews, the Jews are going to think that each one of their three prayer requests has been answered.

1. They are going to say, "This is our long-awaited Messiah."

2. When he confirms the covenant with the Jews for seven years, they will say, "At last, we can live in peace, unharmed by our surrounding enemies."

3. The temple will be rebuilt, and the blood sacrifices will be restored. The Jews will be delighted to think that once again their ceremonial worship can continue.

However, their joy is short-lived. In the middle of the seven-year covenant, Antichrist will turn against the Jews, and the covenant will be broken.

My question to you is this: "Will you choose the Son of God, Jesus Christ, or will you follow History's Greatest Imitator, the Antichrist?

Chapter 7

The Antichrist

In Revelation 13:1–9, under the inspiration of the Holy Spirit, John writes,

> *"And I stood upon the sand of the sea, and saw a Beast rise up out of the sea, having seven heads and ten horns, and upon his horns ten crowns, and upon his heads the name of blasphemy.*
> *And the Beast which I saw was like unto a leopard, and his feet were as the feet of a bear, and his mouth as the mouth of a lion: and the dragon gave him his power, and his seat, and great authority.*
> *And I saw one of his heads as it were wounded to death; and his deadly wound was healed: and all the world wondered after the Beast.*
> *And they worshipped the dragon which gave power unto the Beast: and they worshipped the Beast, saying, Who is like unto the Beast? who is able to make war with him?*
> *And there was given unto him a mouth speaking great things and blasphemies; and power was given unto him to continue forty and two months.*
> *And he opened his mouth in blasphemy against God, to blaspheme his name, and his tabernacle, and them that dwell in Heaven.*
> *And it was given unto him to make war with the saints, and to overcome them: and power was given him over all kindreds, and tongues, and nations.*
> *And all that dwell upon the earth shall worship him, whose names are not written in the book of life of the Lamb slain from the foundation of the world.*
> *If any man have an ear, let him hear."*

The events of Revelation chapter 13 take place midway in the Tribulation period. I believe that the next thing on God's prophetic calendar is what is called the Rapture. I also believe that soon Jesus is coming in the air. Those of us who are saved will be raised to meet Him in the air. Shortly after that time, Antichrist will be revealed to the world. He befriends the Jews according to Daniel 9:26–27, and confirms a covenant with the Jews for seven years. However, in the middle of that seven-year covenant with the Jews, Antichrist breaks the covenant and turns against the Jews. The scene is set for Revelation chapter 13.

When we come to Revelation 13, the first thing we must conclude is that this Beast out of the sea is a man. That is an important fact, because everything in this message is based on that premise. One simple, logical reason that this Beast represents a man is that in the nine verses (Revelation 13:1–9) that describe him, there are no less than eighteen masculine, personal pronouns used in reference to this Beast. Over and over again, the Beast is called "he," "him," "his." The clincher is in verse 18. The number of the Beast is "the number of a man." So, this Beast represents a man. From the passage, notice several things about this Beast out of the sea.

The Description of the Beast

Revelation 13, verses 1 and 2, state that the Beast comes up out of the sea. He has seven heads and ten horns. He is like unto a leopard. He has the feet of a bear and the mouth of a lion. One may say, "Brother Comfort, there is no need for me to read the book of the Revelation. I can't understand it." If you have been saved for a short time, the book of the Revelation is not for you. The book of John is for you. But if you have been saved awhile, and you have a Bible foundation, you will find as you read the book of the Revelation, it usually interprets itself. The best commentary in all the world of Revelation chapter 13 is Revelation chapter 17. We will interpret Revelation 13 in the light of Revelation 17.

Revelation 13, verse one, states that the Beast rises *"…up out of the sea."* Revelation 17:15: *"…the waters which thou sawest…are peoples, and multitudes, and nations, and tongues."* In the Bible, the sea pictures the raging nations as the nations are in political turmoil. A satanically-energized superman, whom the Bible identifies as the Antichrist, will arise from the nations and cause the entire world to worship him.

The Bible says Antichrist has seven heads and ten horns. What are they? The Bible tells us. Notice Revelation 17:9, the middle of the verse. It says, *"The seven heads are seven mountains, on which the woman sitteth."* That is very plain. Most everyone knows that the only major city around the world that sits on seven hills is the city of Rome. Rome will be the political capital of the world in the Tribulation period.

In Revelation 17:10, we read that there are seven kings or kingdoms. In the book of the Revelation, a king represents a kingdom. *"Five are fallen, and one is, and the other is not yet come; and when he cometh, he must continue a short space."* What are those seven kings or kingdoms? There are Bible scholars who say that these seven kings or kingdoms represent seven Roman emperors in succession. I personally do not believe this theory, but rather I believe that as John wrote the Book of Revelation, these seven kings or kingdoms represent seven world governments of the past, the present, and the future that persecuted the Jewish nation. The five that are fallen are these: first there was the Egyptian, replaced by the Assyrian, replaced by the Babylonian, replaced by the Medo-Persian, replaced by the Grecian. Those five world empires had ceased to be when John wrote the book of the Revelation. He said that *"one is."* Rome was in power when John wrote the book of the Revelation. He states, *"...the other is not yet come."* That one that is yet to come will be the revived Roman Empire in the Tribulation period that will comprise the one-world government.

Revelation 17, verse 11, says there is an eighth who is the Beast, and he is of the seven. The eighth is the Antichrist. He is of the seven. That means he is a compilation of those seven world emperors that have preceded him. That draws our attention back to Revelation 13:2, where the Beast is likened unto a leopard, but with the feet of a bear and the mouth of a lion. These animal symbols from the book of Daniel represent various world governments. For instance, this Beast is likened unto a leopard. The leopard prophesies Alexander the Great and all of his military swiftness. He has the feet of a bear. The bear is a strong animal and portrays the Medo-Persian Empire as it came strongly in one night and subdued the Babylonian empire. The Beast has the mouth of a lion. The lion is the king of the jungles and represents the most regal and splendid empire of all times: the Babylonian Empire. Through these word pictures, the Bible is teaching us about the personality of the Antichrist. He will be as swift as Alexander the Great in his military decisions. He will be as strong as Darius the Mede and Cyrus the Persian. He will be as pompous and as splendid as Nebuchadnezzar and Belshazzar. In other words, he will be the most charismatic individual that planet Earth has ever known.

In Daniel 7:8, Antichrist is called the little horn. In Daniel 8:23, he is the king of fierce countenance. In Daniel 9:26, he is the prince that shall come. In Daniel 11:36, he is the willful king. In II Thessalonians 2:3, he is the man of sin and the son of perdition. In II Thessalonians 2:11, he is the lie. In Revelation 9:11, he is the king of the bottomless pit.

Antichrist has seven heads; however, he has ten horns. What are they? In Revelation 17, verse 13, the Bible tells us. *"These (the ten kings) have one mind and shall give their power and strength unto the Beast."* Here you have ten horns representing ten western nations that in the middle of the Tribulation will comprise the one-world government.

There are four blocs of nations that are prominent in the Tribulation. First of all, from Ezekiel 38 and 39, we can identify the kings of the north. In Daniel 11:40, we read of the kings of the south: the Arab and the African nations. Revelation 9:13–21 speaks of the kings of the east as they come over the Euphrates River, two hundred million strong on horseback. These kings represent China, India, and Japan. We are then left to identify the kings or nations of the west. Where is the United States of America geographically? We are in the west. In the west we have professing Christendom. Are you aware that the last battle of the war of Armageddon is when these ten western nations converge upon the Jews to war against the very Son of God from Heaven? I believe the United States of America at the end of the Tribulation period will war against the very One whose name they bear. Professing Christendom will war against the Son of God from Heaven.

The Duration of the Beast

How long will Antichrist's kingdom last? Revelation 13:5 states, *"And power was given him to continue forty and two months."* The kingdom of the Antichrist will last for exactly three and one-half years. At the first half of the Tribulation period, the Antichrist is coming **instead of** Christ. That is what the prefix "anti" means. When the covenant is broken with the Jews at the outset of the last three and one-half years of the tribulation period, he is coming **against** Christ. The prefix "anti" can mean "instead of" or "against." In the first three and one-half years, he is coming instead of Christ, as an imitation of Christ. During the last three and one-half years, he will be the archenemy of Jesus Christ.

In Revelation 19, we read that Jesus is coming back from glory on a white horse. In Revelation 6:1–2, the Antichrist is imitating Jesus Christ on the white horse. Revelation 6:1–2: *"And I saw when the Lamb opened one of the seals, and I heard, as it were the noise of thunder,*

*one of the four Beasts saying, Come and see. And I saw, and behold a
white horse: and he that sat on him had a bow; and a crown was given
unto him: and he went forth conquering, and to conquer."*

The Bible says Antichrist has a bow; however, it does not say he
has an arrow. Why? His victory will be a bloodless victory. It will
not be won on a battlefield; it will be won around a negotiating
table. Antichrist is coming as the white dove of peace. The Bible
says a crown is given unto him, but it does not say he militarily
wins the crown. He wins the affections of the nations, and they
willingly give him the kingdoms of the world. Daniel 11:21, 23,
and 24 state, *"And in his estate shall stand up a vile person, to whom
they shall not give the honour of the kingdom: but he shall come in
peaceably, and obtain the kingdom by flatteries.... And after the league
made with him he shall work deceitfully: for he shall come up, and shall
become strong with a small people. He shall enter peaceably even upon
the fattest places of the provinces."* The key to note in that passage is
this: Antichrist is coming peacefully. He is coming as a politician
with an answer to the world's problems.

It is interesting to note the adjective that is used to describe
Antichrist: a **vile** person. That adjective is used in the Bible to
describe homosexuality. It is my contention that the Antichrist
may very well be a homosexual. The Bible states that he shall not
regard the desire of women (Daniel 11:37). Regardless, he comes in
peaceably and wins the affections of the nations.

In the first three and one-half years of the Tribulation, there
is a semblance of religious toleration, but in the middle of the
Tribulation, religious toleration ceases. In Matthew 24:21–22 Jesus
said, *"For then shall be great tribulation, such as was not since the
beginning of the world to this time, no, nor ever shall be. And except
those days should be shortened, there should no flesh be saved: but for the
elect's sake those days shall be shortened."* Here is an interesting thing:
in Revelation 7, you have the redeemed chorus singing *"Glory and*

honor and blessing to the Lamb that was slain from the foundation of the world," and quite suddenly, the singing stops. There is a deafening silence that pervades all of Heaven. Revelation 8:1 then says, *"There was silence in Heaven about the space of a half an hour."* Why the sudden silence? It is my contention that the redeemed choir and the angelic host are looking down on Earth's scene when the covenant is broken. They stand in stunned silence and disbelief. They cannot believe what their eyes are beholding. The angelic hosts have witnessed every calamity that has ever taken place. In Isaiah 38, one angel in one night slew 185,000 Assyrians. The angelic host looked down on December 7, 1941, when 1,100 men on board the USS Arizona in nine seconds went to a watery grave. They looked down on the Second World War and saw 200,000 people in Okinawa die and because of all the blood spilled in the rivers, the waters actually took on them the color of blood. The angelic host has witnessed every earthquake and every tsunami. However, they have never seen anything to compare with what their eyes are beholding at this time. They stand in stunned silence and disbelief.

Did you know that there is something worse, humanly speaking, than dying? It is to be in so much pain and torment that you want to die to get out of your agony. Revelation 6:15–17: *"And the kings of the earth, and the great men, and the rich men, and the chief captains, and the mighty men, and every bondman, and every free man, hid themselves in the dens and in the rocks of the mountains; And said to the mountains and rocks, Fall on us, and hide us from the face of Him that sitteth on the throne, and from the wrath of the Lamb: For the great day of His wrath is come; and who shall be able to stand?"* Men are going to flee to the mountains, but hail stones will crush the caves. The islands will move out of their places, and men will scream, "Hide us from the face of Him that sits on the throne!" I thank God that I am never going to attend that prayer meeting!

The Dominion of the Beast

Revelation 13:3, latter part of the verse: *"...and all the world wondered after the Beast."* In verse 8: *"...and all that dwell on earth shall worship him."* In verse 12: *"...and he exerciseth all the power of the first Beast and causeth the earth and them which dwell therein to worship the first Beast."* The dominion of the Antichrist will be a worldwide dominion.

Do you have any problem believing that the world is ready to enthrone the Antichrist? From what I read and hear in the news, I have no problem believing that. Listen to this tremendous statement. The mood is well expressed by Henri Spaak, one of the early planners of the common market and former Secretary General of NATO. He said, "We do not want another committee, we have too many already. What we want is a man of sufficient stature to hold the allegiance of all the people, and to lift us out of the economic morass into which we are sinking." He concluded with these words: "Send us such a man, and be he god or be he devil, we will receive him." I contend to you that the world does not care whether it is God or the devil that solves its problems. They just want a superman to resolve their difficulties.

Notice three things that Antichrist's worldwide dominion will encompass. Revelation 17:13 reads, *"These* (or the ten kings) *have one mind, and shall give their power and strength unto the Beast."* His dominion will encompass **a world government.** Just before this transfer of power happens, Russia makes a march down to Jerusalem on horseback according to Ezekiel chapters 38 and 39. When they come down, there will be five nations that will accompany them. From Ezekiel 38:5–6, we learn that Persia is one of those nations. In 1935, the name Persia was changed to Iran. Secondly, there is a country called Ethiopia. Thirdly, there is a country called Libya. Fourthly, there is Gomer, a group identified as the people of Germany. By the way, it used to be fashionable to preach that this was East Germany, but Ezekiel did not say that. Ezekiel said in Ezekiel 38:6: *"...Gomer and all his bands."* So you see, Ezekiel looked into the future and saw the time when the wall would be torn down. There would be no more two Germanys, but one Germany, all of which will be sympathetic with that Northern invasion. There is a disease from which Germany has never recovered, and that disease is Anti-Semitism. For that very reason Germany was against the Iraqi war, because the bottom line to them is Israel and the Jew. Finally, there is a country called Togarmah. These people have been identified as the people of Turkey.

One of the reasons these forces come down is that they see the emergence of the Antichrist, the one-world dictator. They are coming to wrest dominion from him. After Russia has been defeated, it makes way for the ten nations to introduce to the world the one-world dictator. Now again, notice the language of verse 13. It reads, *"These have one mind, and shall give their power and strength unto the Beast."* These words indicate to me that it was not an overnight decision for these ten nations to make the Antichrist the one-world dictator, but there was a conditioning process. The world had to be ready to accept the one-world dictator. It is my contention that such a conditioning process has been going on for hundreds of years. I believe that there has been a person in every time period that could have been the embodiment of the Antichrist, were Jesus to come at that time. Otherwise, if that is not true, the Rapture could not be an imminent event. I believe the Rapture could take place at any time. Therefore, there has always been a person that could have been the embodiment of the Antichrist, had Jesus Christ come during that time.

Turn your attention to a lesson from history. May 1, 1776, thirty-one international financiers met together for the purpose of bringing about a one-world government. They were led by

Adam Weishaupt, who was a professor of canon law at Bavaria University. Adam Weishaupt actually knew what the Bible taught about the Antichrist, and it was his desire to be the embodiment of the Antichrist. He is called the profoundest conspirator that ever lived. He is called a human devil. Go forward many years, and in 1913, the Federal Reserve System was founded in America. You may already be aware that the Federal Reserve System is not part of the United States government. It is actually a group of individual stockholders that arbitrarily make financial decisions that affect the entire world. Income tax was also started in 1913 at the same time as the Federal Reserve System, and the tax was only one percent of the American wage-earners salary! The government knows that the more they tax us the more they control us! Fast forward again to 1920, and the League of Nations was founded to hopefully be the seat of the one-world government. However, the League of Nations was doomed to failure at its inception, because the United States was not behind it. Something cataclysmic had to happen to bring about a world body that would eventually become a world government. That cataclysmic event was the Second World War. After World War II in 1945, the United Nations was founded in New York City, and to ensure that the United States would be a part of that world body, John D. Rockefeller gave the United Nations the property where the United Nations Building sits today.

On Capitol Hill in Washington, the talk is not about **if** we have a world government, but **when** we have a world government. Are you aware that the liberals in our Congress want to make the United States subservient to the United Nations charter? One of the aspects of the United Nations charter is the genocide treaty which states that it will be unlawful one day to convert anybody from their native religion. Our nation is going downhill faster than a toboggan sled toward a one-world government. J. Robert Oppenheimer, the scientist largely responsible for developing the atomic bomb, said, "There must be set a world power." Physicist Arthur Compton said, "World government has become inevitable." Dr. Ralph Perry at Harvard said, "World government is in the making whether we like it or not." The problem is not social; the problem is not moral; the problem is not political; it is spiritual. However, Satan has diverted us to get all excited about these political causes, and in our fervor, we are letting the world die and go to Hell without Jesus Christ.

In Revelation 17:1, we find that the Antichrist's world dominion will also include **a world church.** I give a word of caution here. Though you may not have yet been offended at one thing I have written thus far, and perhaps you would agree with almost everything I have said, at this point, the devil will do his best to get you offended. Please be reminded that I did not write the Bible. I preach the Bible. Religion in America has become a sacred cow. Some say, "All religions are good." If you believe that statement, you would have detested the preaching of Jesus Christ. Simply turn to Matthew 23 where seven times He scathed upon the National Council of Churches of His day. My friend, when the religionists heard Jesus preach, they knew exactly who He had in mind. He did not preach like Robert Schuler, saying, "Everybody is good…and God is good…and nobody is going to be judged." He did not preach that kind of message. He did not say, "There is a certain denomination whose initials start with 'S,' but I'm not going to tell you who they are because I do not want to offend anybody. Oh, and there is another denomination whose initials start with 'P,' but I will not tell you who they are because I do not think you ought to speak ill of another's religion." No, Jesus did not preach that way. He said, *"Woe unto you scribes and Pharisees, Sadducees… hypocrites… whited sepulchers full of dead men's bones."* The liberals say of us, "You fundamentalists are narrow—you don't want unity." I remind you that there is a difference between union and unity. For example, if you take two cats and tie their tails together and throw them over a clothesline, you have a union, but you do not have unity. There is no way that I can sit beside a liberal preacher on the platform of a city-wide meeting in Charlotte, North Carolina, and put my arm around this man who denies that the Bible is the Word of God and call him my Christian brother. He may be a nice man, but my allegiance is not to sympathy; my allegiance is to the Word of God.

Let me give you a Bible principle of interpretation. Whenever you read about a symbolically-impure woman in the Bible such as what we read in Revelation 17:1, she is always symbolic of a false religious system. Notice how God glowingly describes her in the latter part of the verse. He calls her *"the great whore that sitteth upon many waters."* Such flattery! Notice please verse five: *"MYSTERY, BABYLON THE GREAT, THE MOTHER OF HARLOTS AND ABOMINATIONS OF THE EARTH."* Two things can be learned about this woman from that verse. She was born at the tower of Babel. She is a mother, and she has a lot of little children. Do you know who her little children are? They are apostate Baptists. They are apostate Methodists. They are apostate Presbyterians. They are Roman Catholics. They are all congealed into one super Ecumenical Church.

Notice please verse six. This ecumenical church is *"drunken with the blood of the saints, and with the blood of the martyrs of Jesus."* Do you realize that the bride of the Antichrist is going to try to obliterate the name of Jesus Christ from the face of the earth? Some say, "Brother Comfort, I am a Methodist." Sorry, but you are too late for that. There is no such thing as a Methodist anymore. Though you perhaps used to see a church sign reading "Methodist Church," it now reads "United Methodist." One day you will go down the road, and that same church will say "United Protestant." Someday you will go down that same road, and the sign will read "United Catholic."

Verse nine of Revelation 17 states that the woman sits on seven mountains. So not only will Rome be the political capital of the world, but it will also be the religious capital of the world. God has this word of advice for anybody who is in a church that supports the ecumenical movement. Revelation 18:4: *"Come out of her, my people, that ye be not partakers of her sins, and that ye receive not of her plagues."*

In Revelation 13:16–17, we read about a one-world monetary system. *"And he causeth all, both small and great, rich and poor, free and bond, to receive a mark in their right hand, or in their foreheads: And that no man might buy or sell, save he that had the mark, or the name of the Beast, or the number of his name."*

For six years in the late 1970's and early '80's, I lived in Indiana. Our congressman told me a startling thing. He said that in his six years in the Congress, three times a bill was proposed that before a child left the hospital upon birth, that baby should have a mark of the government burned under the first layer of skin on his forehead. He said that on each occasion the bill was defeated, but on each occasion it gained momentum. His prediction was that one day such a bill would be accepted around the world.

I have been reading about the one-world monetary system for many years. The first article I read was in Reader's Digest in 1976. In 1981 as I was on top of the World Trade Center, I saw a monument that said that one day paper money will be obsolete to make way for a new system called Paper Gold. Paper Gold is a misnomer. It is neither paper, nor is it gold. It is like Grapenuts cereal—neither grape nor nuts. It is like Christian Science—neither Christian nor science. In a system using Paper Gold, every country is listed by number on a ledger. That number is denoted as their special drawing rights (SDR). (Incidentally, a man in Kansas City showed me a copy of the *Wall Street Journal*, drawing my attention to the financial listings for the Special Drawing Rights.) The system is supposed to be scaled down from an international to a national to an individual level, where one day every person in the world and every home in the world will have his own SDR or his Personal Identification Number. Before he goes out to buy or sell, he will call into the governing bank giving them his PIN, and a computer will give him authorization to buy or sell for a governed amount of money.

A man in Canada related to me an incident that he saw on the evening news. He said, "Brother Comfort, I was watching about the starvation in India, and I could not believe my eyes. The people were lined up for miles waiting to get food from the government. The one stipulation for receiving food was that the person must have the mark of the government in his right hand, and to get that mark, he had to agree to sterilization. Once he got that mark, he could no longer have children." He said, "Brother Comfort, I thought nobody would take that mark, but I saw people knocking down each other and trampling over bodies just to get the mark of the government in their right hand." My unsaved friend, in the Tribulation period, you will murder to get the mark of the government in your forehead or in your hand. You will murder to be able to buy or sell so you can exist a little bit longer.

The Design of the Beast

Revelation 13, verse 1 says, "*...and upon his heads the name of blasphemy.*" Verse 5: "*...was given unto him a mouth speaking great things and blasphemies.*" Verse 6: "*And he opened his mouth in blasphemy against God.*" The design of Antichrist will be blasphemy. Has there ever been a day in our lifetime when blasphemy was more prevalent than today? A lady in Michigan told me that while shopping in a store, she heard a rock song being played. The song had only two words in it. By the way, if you love rock music, you don't love Jesus Christ. Rock music, with all of its derivatives, is the greatest tool for blasphemy that the devil has ever invented. The lady went on to tell me that the two words in the song were these. The first was "God." The second was a four-letter word of profanity that beings with "d." Over and over and over again those, two words were repeated.

A professor at Purdue University made a survey and found that among the one hundred most-used words in the English language was every word of profanity. He went a step further in his study to discover that one out of five words a factory worker says is a word of profanity. That means that the average factory worker cannot even utter a sentence without using profanity.

Did you ever think that you would live to see the day that in Rocky Mount, North Carolina, in the "Bible Belt," a Methodist church would celebrate a funeral for God? The preacher at the funeral said, "You killed God because you squeezed His hand too tightly." He said, "By the way, God really never did exist. You just created Him out of the fear of your mind."

An issue of *Mad Magazine* pictured Jesus Christ as a shiftless, no-good, marijuana-smoking hippie. God help us! *Hustler* had a series of articles on the sex life of Jesus Christ and of his disciples. God help us! I have seen this cartoon with my own eyes. In Moscow, in one of their leading papers, a flaming cartoon was pictured of which Jesus was the central figure. There were a number of simple-looking individuals around Him, supposedly His disciples, gnawing on His arms and on His legs until there was nothing left but bones. A man, supposedly Peter, was standing at His side filling up a bowl of blood in one hand and drinking a glass of blood with the other hand. Jesus' bowels were severed open, and the disciples were drawing nourishment from His severed bowels. The caption under the cartoon said, "Take, eat, this is my body which is broken for you."

I have in my files, some snapshots of paintings that were on the wall in Pima College, Tucson, Arizona many years ago. This was a display by the art department supposedly to depict religious satire. Many of the pictures I would never describe in a mixed audience. They were shameful. One picture portrayed Jesus Christ, ugly, emaciated, and effeminate, skiing at Miami Beach. A man was drowning and screaming for Jesus to save Him from drowning, but Jesus was oblivious to his call for help. The caption beneath the picture read, "JC does it again at Miami Beach." Another painting portrayed Jesus Christ as a bunny rabbit with a cross on his back. A nude woman is handing an Easter egg to the bunny rabbit and the caption says, "He, the bunny rabbit, died for our sins." How long will God allow this blasphemy to go on?

Revelation 6:9–10: *"And when he had opened the fifth seal, I saw under the altar the souls of them that were slain for the word of God, and for the testimony which they held: And they cried with a loud voice, saying, How long, O Lord, holy and true, dost thou not judge and avenge our blood on them that dwell on the earth?"* When Jesus died on the cross, it was a cry of grace. He said, *"Father, forgive them for they know not what they do."* When they stoned Stephen to death, it was a cry of mercy. He said, *"Lord, lay not this sin to their charge."* However, the saints that are martyred in the Tribulation are not going to be crying for the mercy or the grace of God. They will be crying for the justice and the vengeance of Almighty God. And they will say, *"How long, O Lord, will you let them blaspheme your name and wear out the saints of God?"* Thank God their prayer is soon to be answered.

The Doom of the Beast

In Daniel chapter 2, Nebuchadnezzar had a dream. In his dream he saw a large image made of various metallic substances, all the way from the head of gold to the feet made of clay and iron. Nebuchadnezzar and his Babylonian empire was the head of gold.

The feet made of a mixture of clay and iron speaks of democracy, the last form of government in the Tribulation period. However, the Bible says that there was a Stone cut without hands out of the mountain. That Stone came to the image and smote it, and the image blew to the four winds. Then the Stone set up a kingdom which would last forever and ever.

Who is that Stone cut out of the mountain? It is Jesus Christ. Daniel 7:14: *"And there was given him dominion, and glory, and a kingdom, that all people, nations, and languages, should serve him: his dominion is an everlasting dominion, which shall not pass away, and his kingdom that which shall not be destroyed."*

So armies will come up from the south. They will come down from the north. They will come over from the east and the west, and it looks as if the Jews are going to be obliterated from the face of the earth. But then, the best friend the Jews have ever had comes to their aid—the Lord Jesus Christ Himself. When He comes, He will not come with nuclear weapons. He will not come with atomic warfare. Isaiah 11:4 states, *"…and with the breath of his lips shall he slay the wicked."* Revelation 19:19–20: *"And I saw the Beast, and the kings of the earth, and their armies, gathered together to make war against him that sat on the horse, and against his army. And the Beast was taken, and with him the false prophet that wrought miracles before him, with which he deceived them that had received the mark of the Beast, and them that worshipped his image. These both were cast alive into a lake of fire burning with brimstone."*

We hear much about discrimination today, but do you know who the most-discriminated minority on the face of the earth is? It is not the women, nor the Mexican-Americans. It is fundamental, Bible-believing Christianity. How many times did you hear that Jim Jones was a fundamentalist? What you did not hear was that he was an admitted Marxist who left all of his belongings to the Communist Party. Whenever a person is an idiot and refuses to take his child to the doctor for needed medical attention and lets his child die, the media often says of that person, "He is a fundamentalist." It looks like everything the child of God tries to do is defeated by the onslaughts of Satan. But may I tell you, though it may look like we are losing the battle, we are going to win the war!

A little boy was reading a novel one day and his mother said, "Honey, would you come in and help with the dishes?" He said, "Oh, no, mommy. I can't right now. I'm in the middle of this novel, and the bad man is beating up the good man." She said, "I will give you five minutes, and then you come and help me with the dishes." Five minutes later, he skipped into the kitchen, humming a happy tune. She said, "Honey, I thought you were angry at mama for making you help with the dishes." He said, "Oh, no, mama. When you said I had five minutes, I went to the back of the book and read the last chapter. Mama, it turned out all right! The good man beat up the bad man!" My friend, I have already read the last chapter! One day, God Almighty will take the Antichrist and cast him into a lake of fire! We are more than conquerors through Him Who loved us.

Notice, please, one closing admonition from Revelation 13:9: "*If any man have an ear, let him hear.*" Is this a warning? If you are not sure that you are saved, you need to settle the matter of salvation immediately, because, my friend, you will not have the opportunity for salvation in the Tribulation period. You have heard the Word of God now; you will not have a chance in the Tribulation period. Because of the truth of this Bible message, the only thing that is important in life is serving Jesus Christ.

Chapter 8
The Reality of Hell

Luke 16:19–31:

"There was a certain rich man, which was clothed in purple and fine linen, and fared sumptuously every day:
And there was a certain beggar named Lazarus, which was laid at his gate, full of sores,
And desiring to be fed with the crumbs which fell from the rich man's table: moreover the dogs came and licked his sores.
And it came to pass, that the beggar died, and was carried by the angels into Abraham's bosom: the rich man also died, and was buried;
And in Hell he lift up his eyes, being in torments, and seeth Abraham afar off, and Lazarus in his bosom.
And he cried and said, Father Abraham, have mercy on me, and send Lazarus, that he may dip the tip of his finger in water, and cool my tongue; for I am tormented in this flame.
But Abraham said, Son, remember that thou in thy lifetime receivedst thy good things, and likewise Lazarus evil things: but now he is comforted, and thou art tormented.
And beside all this, between us and you there is a great gulf fixed: so that they which would pass from hence to you cannot; neither can they pass to us, that would come from thence.
Then he said, I pray thee therefore, father, that thou wouldest send him to my father's house:
For I have five brethren; that he may testify unto them, lest they also come into this place of torment.
Abraham saith unto him, They have Moses and the prophets; let them hear them.
And he said, Nay, father Abraham: but if one went unto them from the dead, they will repent.
And he said unto him, If they hear not Moses and the prophets, neither will they be persuaded, though one rose from the dead."

There are some that would have you believe that this story is a parable. Most of the time, those who believe that error have an ulterior motive of doing away with the reality of Hell. There are several reasons why I do not believe that this is a parable. The obvious reason is that in any parable or story that Jesus ever told, He never gave proper nouns. In this story, you have Moses, you have Lazarus, and you have Abraham. But let's concede for the sake of argument that this **is** a parable. What is a parable? A parable is an earthly story with a Heavenly meaning. A parable is an illustration of a real thing. If this is a parable, and I don't believe that it is, then it still does not do away with the reality of Hell because it is simply a picture of something that is real.

Two things must be kept in mind as one reads this story. First, who was it that told the story? It was none other than Jesus Christ. Are you aware that for every one time that Jesus described Heaven in Scripture, He described Hell at least ten times? In the New Testament, there are two hundred sixty-two chapters. No less than two hundred thirty chapters teach the doctrine of eternal punishment. It was Jesus that told this story. Perhaps the hottest sermon that ever fell from the lips of any man came from the lips of Jesus Christ. In Mark 9:43–48 He said, *"And if thy hand offend thee, cut it off: it is better for thee to enter into life maimed, than having two hands to go into hell, into the fire that never shall be quenched: Where their worm dieth not, and the fire is not quenched. And if thy foot offend thee, cut it off: it is better for thee to enter halt into life, than having two feet to be cast into hell, into the fire that never shall be quenched: Where their worm dieth not, and the fire is not quenched. And if thine eye offend thee, pluck it out: it is better for thee to enter into the kingdom of God with one eye, than having two eyes to be cast into hell fire: Where their worm dieth not, and the fire is not quenched."* It was Jesus that told this story.

The second thing that you must bear in mind regarding the story in Luke 16 is this: to whom was the story spoken? I do not believe that you can have a proper understanding of this passage without a key that unlocks the door. What is that key? Luke 16, verse 15. Rarely will you hear this passage preached with verse 15 related to it. I do not believe you can have a proper understanding of this scripture without including verse 15. *"And He said unto them, Ye are they which justify yourselves before men; but God knoweth your hearts: for that which is highly esteemed among men is abomination in the sight of God."* Jesus is talking to people who justify themselves before men: religious people. He goes on to relate His story to them about a man who justified himself before men—a religious man, if you please. Here is an interesting thing about the pattern of Jesus' preaching. When Jesus preached to the down-and-outer, He did not primarily preach about Hell, but He preached about love. For instance, do you remember when He came to the town of Jericho? He approached Zacchaeus, the most hated man in the entire town. Publicans were hated people; but Zacchaeus was not simply a publican—he was the chief among the publicans. That tells me that he was doubly-hated over anybody in town. But Jesus did not preach Hell to Zacchaeus that day. In Luke 19:5, it says, *"And when Jesus came to the place, He looked up, and saw him, and said unto him, Zacchaeus, make haste, and come down; for to day I must abide at thy house."* That day, Zacchaeus was saved, because he found Somebody Who loved him.

Recall the story from John 4. A woman came to the well at midday to draw water. Women normally did not come at midday to draw water. They would usually come early in the morning or late at night. Why? Because at midday, they were busy taking care of their household chores. It is my contention that this woman came at midday to seek a man. She had been married five times, and she was living in adultery with a man that was not her husband. Jesus did not preach Hell to this scarlet woman; he preached love. In

John 4:13–14, He said, *"Whosoever drinketh of this water shall thirst again: But whosoever drinketh of the water that I shall give him shall never thirst; but the water that I shall give him shall be in him a well of water springing up into everlasting life."* That day, the town harlot drank at the springs of living water, because she found Someone Who loved her.

Recall yet another story from John 8 of a woman taken in the very act of adultery. Adultery demanded stoning, and as the accusers gathered around and point their fingers at the woman, the Bible says that Jesus reached over and wrote something in the sand. We are not told what He wrote. Do you remember another incident in the Bible where the finger of God wrote something? What about the writing of the The Ten Commandments? It very well could be that Jesus just wrote the Ten Commandments in the sand, for by the law is the knowledge of sin. Whatever He wrote in the sand convicted the accusers in their hearts, and He said to the woman in John 8:10–11: *"…hath no man condemned thee? She said, No man, Lord. And Jesus said unto her, Neither do I condemn thee: go, and sin no more."* And that day the scarlet woman was made pure, because she found Someone Who loved her.

On the other hand, when Jesus Christ preached to the religious crowd, He did not preach about love to that crowd. He preached about Hell and He preached it very warmly! For instance, in Matthew 23, seven times He scathed upon the National Council of Churches of His day. He said, *"Woe unto you, scribes and Pharisees, hypocrites!…whited sepulchres…full of dead men's bones…."* Matthew 23:15: *"for ye compass sea and land to make one proselyte, and when he is made, ye make him twofold more the child of Hell than yourselves."* I would say that is strong preaching! In Matthew 23:33, Jesus said, *"Ye serpents, ye generation of vipers, how can ye escape the damnation of Hell?"*

I try to follow Jesus' pattern of preaching in my own ministry. When I go to a jail, on occasion, and preach to men behind bars, I do not spend a long time telling them that they are on their way to Hell. They know that. I do not spend a long time telling them that they are sinners. The bars they stand behind tell them that they are sinners. I mention sin, but the burden of my message is that Someone took their Hell on Calvary's cross, and because He loved them, they do not have to go to Hell. On the other hand, when I preach to people who think that they are going to get to Heaven by going through the baptistry or by partaking of the seven sacraments or by being sprinkled as a baby, I preach on Hell, and I preach it very warmly.

The word that is translated "Hell" in Luke 16:23 is the word "Hades." Hades and the Lake of Fire are not the same. They are alike in many ways, but they are not the same. Let me differentiate. When a person without Christ dies today, he goes to Hell (Hades). Everyone suffers alike in Hades. There is no degree of punishment in Hades. However, Revelation 20:12 says that one day all of those who are in Hades will be bodily resurrected to stand before the Great White Throne Judgment. It is already a foregone conclusion that everyone who is judged at the Great White Throne will be cast into the Lake of Fire. You may say, "Then why are they standing there?" They are standing there to receive their degree of punishment in the Lake of Fire. Psalm 62:12: *"Also unto thee, O Lord, belongeth mercy: for thou renderest to every man according to his work."* Jeremiah 17:10: *"I the LORD search the heart, I try the reins, even to give every man according to his ways, and according to the fruit of his doings."* Romans 2:6: *"Who will render to every man according to his deeds:"* Romans 2:16: *"In the day when God shall judge the secrets of men by Jesus Christ according to my gospel."*

In summary, when a person dies today without Christ, he goes to Hades. Everyone suffers alike in Hades. One day all of those who are in Hades will be resurrected to stand before the Great White Throne Judgment. At that time, they will receive their degree of punishment in the Lake of Fire. Although Hades and the Lake of Fire are not the same, they are alike in many ways. I want to point out four things about the word that is translated Hell.

Hell Is a Place for Sinners.

Notice Luke 16, verses 19–21. Can you find one moral indictment that is given against this rich man? Does it say he was a drunkard? Does it say he was a drug addict? Does it say he was a blasphemer? You may say, "Well, I found something wrong with him. The poor man lay at his gate full of sores, and all that the rich man gave him was crumbs to eat." May I draw something to your attention? The word for gate means a place of artistry or beauty. The word sores means pus-filled sores. I believe that poor Lazarus thought, "No one will let me mess up their landscaping and lie at their beautiful gate with these kinds of sores. Yet, I know one man that will. Few people will give me something to eat. Yet, I know one man who will." If you have ever viewed the film "The Burning Hell," you would likely agree that it is a good soul-winning film in many aspects. However, I think the film misses a very strategic point. The film pictures the rich man as a drunkard, a reprobate, and a blasphemer. You do not find that in the context. I think everything in the context is to the commendation and not to the condemnation of this rich man. This was a man who justified himself before men.

You may well ask then, "If he was such a good man, why did he die and go to Hell?" The only reason anybody ever dies and goes to Hell is that he simply rejected God's Son, the Lord Jesus Christ. John 3:18: *"He that believeth on him is not condemned: but he that believeth not is condemned **already**…."* Unsaved friend, you are not going to be condemned when you go to Hell; you are condemned at this moment. John 3:36: *"He that believeth on the Son hath everlasting life: and he that believeth not the Son shall not see life; but the wrath of God* (present tense) *abideth on him."* The wrath of God swings over the head of an unsaved person like a pendulum and is ready to devour that unsaved person at any time. In Jonathan Edwards' sermon, "Sinners in the Hands of an Angry God," he said this: "God is under no obligation to keep the sinner out of Hell one second." The more I think about that statement, the more that it burns into my heart. For fifteen years of my life, I shook my fist in the face of God. I said, "God, hands off of my life! You are not going to tell me how to live!" Yet, every breath that I breathed was by the grace of God. Let me say, my dear unsaved friend, God holds the last breath of your life in His hands. He can snuff it out any time that He sees fit.

As I contemplate the rich man, I note a very sad thing. Here is a moral, upright man in Hell tonight, with the rogue's gallery of sinners of all the ages. Do you know that God gives us an idea of what the phone directory in Hell will be like? Revelation 21:8 is what I call "Hell's Phone Directory." Notice the listings: *"But the fearful, and unbelieving, and the abominable, and murderers, and whoremongers, and sorcerers, and idolaters, and all liars, shall have their part in the lake which burneth with fire and brimstone: which is the second death."*

God lists for us eight classifications of people in Revelation 21 verse 8. Who is the first one? **The fearful.** Do you know who that is? That is the teenager who lives under the domination of the peer group—afraid to get saved, afraid he may get laughed at by the peer group. That is a barrel-chested, beer-drinking man who is afraid to get saved. He is afraid that his buddies will say, "Here comes Mr. Old-time Religion." The most prevalent reason why a person dies and goes to Hell: P-R-I-D-E. Many that sit in church are afraid to come forward to truly trust Christ as Savior fearing, "What will people think of me? My pastor thinks I'm saved. I was the best, the finest Christian in the youth group. What will they think of me?" The most prevalent reason people die and go to Hell is pride.

Who is the second listing in the phone directory? **The unbeliever.** Do you know who that is? That is a person who keeps the Golden Rule. The Ten Commandment-keeper. However he dies without Jesus Christ. That is a Methodist or Baptist Sunday School teacher who dies without Jesus Christ.

Who is the moral unbeliver's next-door neighbor in Hell? **The abominable.** How many of you remember the name John Wayne Gacy? Many years ago, perhaps the most abominable thing that has been done in my lifetime took place in Chicago, Illinois. John Wayne Gacy sodomized and murdered thirty-three young men and buried them under his garage floor. Would you move into a community knowing that John Wayne Gacy is your next-door neighbor? But here is the moral unbeliever right next door to the Saddam Husseins, the Adolf Hitlers, and the John Wayne Gacys.

If you go down the block a short way, you find **the sorcerer.** The Greek word for sorcerer is the same word from which we get the word pharmacy. *Pharmakeus*—drugs. So just down the block from John Wayne Gacys and the murderers of the ages, we find a man on a bad LSD trip and perhaps another screaming for a fix of heroin. But right in the midst of this rogue's gallery of sinners is the moral unbeliever. My friend, you do not want to go there.

Someone said, "Well, a person will be different when he goes to Hell than he was in life." Do you believe that? Revelation 22:11: *"He that is unjust, let him be unjust still: and he which is filthy, let him be filthy still:...."* I believe that Hell is a place of unbridled passions and unfulfilled desires. I believe that as a person is in life, so he is in Hell. Have you ever seen a person suffering from DT's—Delirium Tremens? Can you imagine a person dying and going to Hell and his entire body convulsing and craving a drop of liquor, but he will never get it? I believe that the harlot will still have a harlot's heart in Hell. She will try to sell the lust of her flesh, but no one will be able to buy it. I believe that if you and I went down the halls of Hell, we would see Pontius Pilate trying to wash the blood of Jesus Christ from his hands. For all eternity he will be washing. I believe if you and I could go down the halls of Hell, we would see Judas Iscariot with his thirty pieces of silver fiendishly screaming, "I betrayed innocent blood! I betrayed innocent blood!" If you and I could go down the halls of Hell, I believe we would see Queen Jezebel with the blood of Naboth dripping from her hands screaming, "I killed him! I killed him!" Hell is a place of unbridled passions and unfulfilled desires.

Hell Is a Place of Suffering.

Notice Luke 16, verse 23 where it says, *"And in Hell he lift up his eyes, being in torments,..."* verse 24, latter part of the verse *"for I am tormented in this flame."* Verse 25, latter part of the verse *"and thou art tormented."* Look ahead to verse 28 *"...lest they also come into this place of torment."* Do you know what the word "torment" means? Hell is identified as a place of severe pain or continuous torture. Think of that! I wish I could preach like our Seventh Day Adventist Day friends preach that one day Hell is going to burn up, and it is going to cease to be. How I wish I could preach that! But Jesus did not say that. Matthew 25:41: *"Then shall he say also unto them on the left hand, Depart from me, ye cursed, into everlasting fire, prepared for the devil and his angels:"* Matthew 25:46: *"And these shall go away into everlasting punishment: but the righteous into life eternal."* Revelation 14:10–11 *"The same shall drink of the wine of the wrath of God, which is poured out without mixture into the cup of his indignation; and he shall be tormented with fire and brimstone in the presence of the holy angels, and in the presence of the Lamb: And the smoke of their torment ascendeth up for ever and ever: and they have no rest day nor night...."*

The phrase "forever and ever" is a very interesting phrase. It is used twenty times in the New Testament. You can prove the eternality of Hell solely on the basis of the phrase "forever and ever." Sixteen times when the phrase is used it describes the eternality of God. When I think of God, I like to think of God as a circle. Where does a circle begin? It has no beginning. Where does a circle end? It has no ending. That is God! Micah 5:2: *"... whose goings forth have been from of old, from everlasting."* Psalm 90:2: *"Before the mountains were brought forth, or ever thou hadst formed the earth and the world, even from everlasting to everlasting, thou art God."*

Sixteen times the phrase "forever and ever" describes the eternality of God. Three times it describes the eternality of Hell. Mr. Jehovah's Witness, you tell me Hell is not forever and ever. Logically then, you have to tell me neither is God, because the same phrase describes both. Sixteen times it describes the eternality of God, three times the eternality of Hell, only one time does it describe the eternality of Heaven. Perhaps you, like I, have gone to a funeral when everyone was aware that the body in the casket was the body of a man who was a reprobate—a God-hater. What did the liberal preacher do? He preached the reprobate straight into the gates of God. He went to lengths talking about the beauties of Heaven and, in the same breath, denied the existence of Hell. Excuse me, that is not being an intellectual, but rather that is being an ignoramus.

When I was in college, I had a course in philosophy. I called it "Fool-osophy." It was the biggest bore and waste of time in my entire college career. However, I did learn something in Philosophy class. Every philosopher realized this: "Every thesis is contradicted by an antithesis." What does that mean? It means everything has its opposite. In other words, there can be no North without South. There can be no East without West. There can be no right without wrong. There can be no black without white. Everything has its opposite. If there is no Hell, then there is no Heaven. If there is a Heaven, that necessitates there must be a Hell. I hear some say, "Well, even if there is no Heaven to gain, I am still glad that I am saved." Paul did not say that. I Corinthians 15:19: *"If in this life only we have hope in Christ, we are of all men most miserable."* Paul said that if there is no Heaven to gain, we are the biggest fools on the face of the earth. But, there is a Heaven to gain and that necessitates there must be a Hell to shun.

In the Luke 16 passage of Scripture, God has taken the minor details of this story to point out the terribleness of the suffering in Hell. Man learns and relates to his surroundings by his senses. Every sense that this rich man had in life, he has in Hell—every sense. I once read a book of over three hundred pages by a godly man named I. M. Haldeman. I agreed with everything he said in all those pages, except one thing. He said that when a person dies and goes to Hell, he is a disembodied spirit—his spirit suffers, but not his body. Let me remind you of Mark 9:43–48 *"…two hands in Hell, two feet in Hell, two eyes in Hell."* Matthew 10:28: *"And fear not them which kill the body, but are not able to kill the soul: but rather fear him which is able to destroy both soul and body in Hell."*

Every sense that the rich man had in life, he has in Hell. Verse 23 says, *"…and in Hell he lift up his eyes…"* There is the sense of sight. *"…being in torments…"* He has the sense of feeling. *"…and he seeth…"* He sees. Verse 24: *"…and he cried…"* He has emotion. *"…and he said…"* He has the ability to speak. The latter part of the verse says, *"…cool my tongue…"* He has the sense of taste. *"…for I am tormented…"* Again we note the sense of feeling. And in verse 25: *"…Abraham said…"* He has the sense of hearing. Every sense he had in life, he has in Hell.

One may say, "But wait, this is not the lake of fire. This is Hades. His body is in the ground awaiting the resurrection. How can he have a physical body in Hades when his body is in the ground awaiting the resurrection?" I do not know all the answers, but I do believe that there is never a time when our spirits are not clothed upon by some type of a body. II Corinthians 5:1: *"For we know that if our earthly house of this tabernacle were dissolved, we have* (present tense) *a building of God, an house not made with hands, eternal in the Heavens."* I believe that there is an intermediary body awaiting the resurrection. Do you remember when Peter, James, and John went up to the mount of Transfiguration? Who did they see on the mount? Moses and Elijah. You may say, "I know why. Elijah went to Heaven without dying." Yes, but what about Moses. Moses died on Mount Nebo and God buried him. Yet on the mount, before he was resurrected, he had a recognizable body.

Again, note how God uses the minute details of this story to point out the terribleness of the suffering in Hell. In life, the rich man was clothed in purple and fine linen. A robe of purple and fine linen was worth six times its weight in gold! Do you know what that tells me about this man? He was a multi-millionaire. He rode the finest chariots of his day. He wore the finest robes of his day. He was waited on hand and foot. But then the scene changes, and he dies and goes to Hell. When he dies and goes to Hell, for what does he ask? Does he ask for servants? No. Does he ask for his palace? No. At one time I thought that he asked for a drop of water, but in actuality he asked for much less than that. If you put your finger in water and pull it back, you are going to come back with a whole lot less than a drop of water. Ponder this interesting thought. There is a multi-millionaire in Hell this very day screaming for an infinitesimal amount of water, but he will never get it. Zechariah 9:11 says that there is no water in the pit.

I do not know what the intermediary body will entail, but I do know that it will suffer. Perhaps it may be somewhat like this illustration. Years ago I was in Colorado for a meeting and the pastor said, "Brother Comfort, there is a man in my church that had his arm cut off yesterday. Would you go with me to the hospital to see the man?" So he and I stood in that hospital room looking, but trying not to look, at that bloody nub. The longer I stood there, the sicker I became. I have a weak stomach and do not do well with the sight of blood. I knew that if I did not leave that room soon something bad was going to happen. I knew I had to leave the room, but before I did, the man looked at me and said, "Preacher, do you know what is the worst thing about this mishap? It is not that I lost my arm. The worst thing about it is that my arm keeps itching me. I reach over to scratch it, but it is not there. It is about to drive me out of my mind."

In 1974, I was in a meeting at Davidson Memorial Baptist Church on Route 74 in Shelby, North Carolina, long before I ever thought about Ambassador Baptist College or living in Shelby. I stood in the home of a man whose leg had been amputated six months before. He said, "Preacher, you will think this is stupid, but that leg that I had amputated six months ago—the calf of that leg is cramped. I reach down to soothe the cramped muscle, but it is just not there. It is about to drive me out of my mind." I mentioned this encounter in a church in Indianapolis and a nurse came to me and said, "Brother Comfort, what you have preached is valid. Whenever we have an amputation in the hospital, that amputee has some type of a burning, itching, or cramping sensation in the amputated limb. On their hospital chart we write, 'Phantom Pains.'" Phantom pains. Can you imagine dying and going to Hell and reaching over to soothe your tormented body, but it's just not there?

Hell Is a Place of Sorrow

Continuing to Luke 16, verse 24, we find that Hell is a place of sorrow. "*...And he **cried** and said,*"—a place of sorrow. Matthew 13:41–42: "*The Son of man shall send forth his angels, and they shall gather out of his kingdom all things that offend, and them which do iniquity; And shall cast them into a furnace of fire: there shall be **wailing and gnashing of teeth.**"*

Many years ago, when I was a college student, my brother and I visited my mother in Creedmoor Hospital on Long Island. My mother spent thirty-five to forty years in mental institutions all over New York and Pennsylvania. As my brother and I walked down the halls of this hospital, we heard the weirdest screams and cries that I have ever heard in my life. These screams and cries pierced through my body like an arrow. I could not wait to get out of that place. As we left, I looked at my brother and said, "Billy, I believe that God has given us just a tiny picture of what Hell must be like." Can you imagine going to a place where the screams of the damned ascend from the sulphuric avenues of Hell, and they have no rest day or night? A place of sorrow.

I mention three reasons why I believe there is sorrow in Hell. First of all, notice verse 25: "*But Abraham said, 'Son, remember....'"* Remember. I think **remembrance** must be a terrible thing in Hell. This rich man is in Hell tonight remembering his palace. He remembers his upstanding position in the community. He remembers his luxuries, his chariots, and his servants. All of those comforts are absent in Hell. Do you not think that remembering would add to his torment in Hell? Notice what Abraham called him. He called him "*son.*" I believe that word was a bolt from the blue. When Abraham addressed him as son, I believe he was reminded of every opportunity he had to receive the Messiah. He is an unsaved son of Abraham in Hell. It was unto the Jews that the oracles of God were committed. John 1:11–12: "*He came unto*

his own, and his own received him not. But as many as received him,
to them gave he power to become the sons of God.…" I believe that as
this rich man is in Hell tonight his memory rehearses all of those
opportunities he had to receive the Messiah. The Bible does not
say, but this man very well may have sat on the shores of Galilee
when Jesus fed the five thousand. How do you think it would
be to die and go to Hell having heard the Son of God preach,
having seen the miracles fall from his hands? In Hell tonight, I
believe, he says, "Can I ever get away from those burning eyes
and that thunderous voice? Can I ever get away from the vision
of Jesus Christ?" Can you imagine a person dying and going to
Hell having sat in a revival meeting and in Hell forever and ever
hearing, "Just as I am without one plea, but that Thy blood was
shed for me, and that Thou biddest me come to thee, oh Lamb
of God, I come." I believe that the sinner in Hell will say, "Stop
the music! Stop the music! Won't that song ever quit playing?"
Memory must be a terrible thing in Hell.

Hell is a place of sorrow because of the **influence** you may have
had to take others with you to that awful place. Remember
Romans 14:7–8: *"For none of us liveth to himself, and no man dieth*
to himself. For whether we live, we live unto the Lord; and whether
we die, we die unto the Lord: whether we live therefore, or die, we are
the Lord's." Anybody who dies and goes to Hell will influence
somebody to go to Hell with him. Some say of the rich man, "Here
is a soul-winner in Hell!" Excuse me, I do not believe that. I have
heard missionaries preach, "Here is a missionary-minded man in
Hell." Was he a missionary-minded man in life? Was he a soul-
winner in life? As a man is in life, so he is in Hell. You may ask,
"Why then did he not want his five brothers to go to Hell?" Here
is my contention: I believe that in his family there were six boys
of which he was the oldest. Every parent has seen how the oldest
child sets the example for the other children in the family.

When my daughters were growing up, my middle daughter Becky always wanted to be like her older sister, Ronda. Ronda was the apple of Becky's eyes. When Becky was approaching her fourth birthday, Ronda was already five years old. We came to Becky and said, "Becky, what gift do you want for your fourth birthday?" She said, "Daddy, I would like to be five years old like Ronda. I would like to have long hair like Ronda—and I would like to **be** Ronda." When going to a restaurant, the waitress would come to take our order. Ronda would place her order first. Then, the waitress would ask Becky what she wanted, and Becky would say, "I want whatever Ronda ordered." I believe there was a time that if Ronda jumped off the roof of the church auditorium, Becky would have said, "Daddy, can I do it? Ronda did it." Becky wanted to do everything that Ronda did.

Here is my contention regarding the rich man's seeming concern for his brother. I believe that this man knew that as he lived, so his five younger brothers were going to live. He knew that as he died, so his five younger brothers were going to die. He knew that when they got to Hell, they were going to point to him throughout all eternity and say, "Brother, it's your fault! Brother, it's your fault!" The billion-degree flames of Hell will be nothing compared to a son or daughter pointing to a mom or dad and saying, "Momma, it's your fault. Daddy, it's your fault."

There is sorrow in Hell because it is a place of **darkness**. II Peter 2:4 calls it *"chains of darkness."* In II Peter 2:17, it is *"mist of darkness."* In Jude 13, it is *"blackness of darkness."* In Matthew 8:12, it is called *"outer darkness."* Someone says, "How in the world could there be fire in Hell, and it be a place of darkness?" Ask any member of the fire department what equipment is taken with him when going into a home to put out a fire. A flashlight is always a part of his gear. In a burning house there is fire, but also darkness.

Hell is a place of outer darkness, chains of darkness, mist of darkness, and blackness of darkness.

Hell Is a Place of Separation.

In our text in Luke 16, notice verse 26. Abraham says, *"And beside all this, between us and you there is a great gulf fixed: so that they which would pass from hence to you cannot; neither can they pass to us, that would come from thence."* I wonder what this rich man would have said if Abraham had looked over and said, "Sir, if you are a good man in Hell, in one million years I am going to let you out of Hell for five minutes. In that five minutes, I am going to give you the biggest drink of water that you have ever had in your entire life." Do you know what I believe the rich man in Hell would have said? "Oh, I must stay away from the harlots. I must stay away from the dirty-joke-telling crowd. I cannot be around that crowd, because if I am a good man in Hell, then in one million years, I will be able to get out for five minutes." However, Abraham did not give that option. He said, "Son, you are in Hell, and Hell is a place of no repentance and no return."

Have you ever thought about this? There are three things that are the same about Heaven and Hell:
1. There is no exit from either place.
2. The inhabitants will be there forever.
3. They last the same amount of time.

Think with me about three things from which the lost man in Hell is separated. First, he is **separated from the good things of life.** Recall Luke 16, verse 25. *"...remember that thou in thy lifetime receivedst thy good things."* There are no good things in Hell. There are no chandeliers. There is no air conditioning. There are no Cadillacs in Hell. All of the good things of earth are absent. No granddaddy will be able to take his grandson on his lap and hear that grandson say, "Paw-Paw, I love you." No mother will be able to clutch that little baby to her bosom and feel the warm breath of that baby on her cheek. One will never hear the laughter of a little baby in Hell. All of the good things of life will be absent from Hell.

Secondly, the lost man in Hell is **separated from his loved ones**. I've heard people say this, "If my husband dies and goes to Hell, because I love him so much, I want to die and go to Hell with him." That is a foolish thing to say. I believe that in Hell every person is an island to himself. There will be no concourse among those who are in Hell.

I loved my Dad with all my heart. I truly believe that I would have been willing to go to Hell in my father's place. Many years ago, I was preaching in Jacksonville, North Carolina. My wife was at home expecting a baby, so I was alone. After preaching a message on the subject of compassion, I went to my motel and wrote my dad a tear-stained letter. I wrote, "Dad, as I am writing to you right now, tears are streaming down my face. I have shed thousands of tears over your soul. I have prayed thousands of prayers over your soul. I cannot stand the thought of your dying and going to Hell." I saw my dad the next summer after he had suffered three heart attacks. All the vim, vigor, and vitality that I knew and loved in my dad were gone. I thought to myself, "The next time I see my dad, I may be standing over his casket to preach his funeral." What could I say about my dad, knowing that his body was in the casket but his soul was in Hell? What could I say about him? I said to my dad, "Dad, I love you so much. I see that you're failing. You may not have much time left on this earth." He said, "Son, you're right." But he did not get saved. The next summer, as I was at the Bill Rice Ranch preparing to go to the Tabernacle to preach, someone handed me my mail. In the mail was a letter from my stepmother. My stepmother was illiterate. Although she could read numbers, she really could not read or write. A friend had penned the letter for her. The letter read this:

"Dear Ronnie, your daddy has been taken to the hospital. He has lost over forty-five pounds. His larynx is swollen. He cannot swallow any food; he cannot hold down any food. We do not know why, but we have to find out." If you knew that your father had lived a life of drinking, smoking, and carousing, what would have been your first thought? I felt for certain that the prognosis would not be good. I feared lung cancer. You have no idea how heavy my heart was when I went to the Tabernacle that morning, knowing that before the closing "Amen" was said, my daddy might be in Hell.

I prayed for my dad for thirty-three years. On Monday night, June 23, 1986, during a meeting I was preaching at Emmanuel Baptist Church in Mechanicsburg, Pennsylvania, my Dad came down the aisle and was born again. Pastor Don Smith knelt at the front row and led him to Christ. I thank God that I could stand over my dad's casket in January, 1989, and say, "Folks, there is no question mark over my daddy's casket, because on June 23, 1986, after thirty-three years of praying for him, my dad came down the aisle and received Christ." Have you ever shed one tear over your unsaved loved one's soul? Have you ever fasted one meal because your loved one meant more to you than the food on your table? I thank God that I will not be separated from my dad for all eternity.

However, the worst suffering of all in Hell is that those who are there are forever **separated from God**. Revelation 22:5 says that in Heaven, we will have no need of the sun, moon, or stars because Jesus is the light in that new city. Hell is termed "outer darkness" because the "light of the world"—the Lord Jesus Christ—is not there. You can take the John Wayne Gacys, the Saddam Husseins, and the billion-degree flames out of Hell, yet it will still be Hell. The worst thing about Hell is that those who are there will be separated from God and His love forever.

In the late 1960's, my family and I lived in Clarksburg, West Virginia. I had just returned from the Bible Lands, and a local church in the area had asked me to show my slides on the Bible Lands for their Wednesday evening service. My wife and daughters went to our own local church to prayer meeting that night. How I thank God that my wife and my family were not with me! I fellowshipped with the pastor for whom I preached, and at about 11 o'clock at night, I started for home. In those days, I struggled with an eye disease that I had been told would eventually cause blindness. I had 20/400 vision in both eyes, and I am told that 20/200 vision is declared legally blind. Thus night driving was not the easiest for me, but I had not yet been restricted. (God has since preserved my vision through two corneal transplants and three cataract procedures.) That night, however, I stopped to pick up my nephew to bring him home with me. It had been raining all day long, and as we left the lighted streets and the city limits, it did not seem that the headlights penetrated the darkness at all. Suddenly, staggering in front of my car was a drunken man, and before I had time to react, I hit him. He flew over the hood of my car and landed under the wheels. The first thing I thought was, "This is a nightmare—it could not happen to me." Then I thought, "Someone has played a trick on me and thrown an object in my pathway." I immediately stopped the car. I ran around to the side, and there under the wheels of my car was a man with gaping mouth. His eyes were closed. I got down on my knees close to his ear and said, "Sir, you don't have much time. You need to get ready to meet the Lord."

Because the accident happened in a very close proximity to the local hospital, the ambulance arrived almost immediately. A nurse came near to me and said, "Sir, you don't have to talk to him. He is already dead. He cannot hear you." I never had a vision of Hell so clearly as I got that night. Here was a man that had lived twenty years in a shack in the middle of nowhere. His wife had left him twenty years before. This man would go into town early in the morning, drink anything with alcohol in it, and stagger home late at night. The only possession he had on his person that night was a bottle of hair tonic that he had been drinking. In a few days, when my wife and I went to the funeral home shortly before his funeral, only two people had signed the guest register—his daughter and his son-in-law. As far as I know, his wife did not even come to his funeral. The night of the accident, the sheriff, noting that I was visibly shaken, tried to reassure me. He told me how frequently he had been called to come and take the man home. He said, "Please do not fault yourself. I knew that some night I was going to get the fatal phone call that the man had been hit by a car." However, as I looked at that man under the wheels of my car, nothing the sheriff said could comfort my heart. I said, "Dear God, I deserve to be where this man is right now. But by your grace, I would be where this man is at this moment. Lord, I want every drop of blood in my body dedicated to keeping people out of the place where this man is tonight."

Had you been the one under the wheels of my car, where would you spend eternity?

Last Things

Chapter 9

The Great White Throne Judgment

Revelation 20:11–15. John writes,

> *"And I saw a great white throne, and him that sat on it, from whose face the earth and the Heaven fled away; and there was found no place for them.*
> *And I saw the dead, small and great, stand before God; and the books were opened: and another book was opened, which is the book of life: and the dead were judged out of those things which were written in the books, according to their works.*
> *And the sea gave up the dead which were in it; and death and Hell delivered up the dead which were in them: and they were judged every man according to their works.*
> *And death and Hell were cast into the lake of fire. This is the second death.*
> *And whosoever was not found written in the book of life was cast into the lake of fire."*

As I begin this message, I am going to be very candid with you. You are going to read a very poor explanation of this passage of scripture. If I had a tongue dipped in the ink of Heaven and command over all of the descriptive adjectives in the English language, my oratory would fall short of adequately describing this passage.

What I would like to do by way of introduction is to give you a Bible panorama of prophecy leading up to the events of Revelation chapter 20. I believe that the next thing on God's prophetic calendar is the Rapture. I frequently hear this statement: "Every day we are seeing Scriptures fulfilled before our eyes." Pardon me, but that is not true. We are seeing shadows of fulfilled prophecies. The next prophecy that will be fulfilled will be the

Rapture of the church. I Thessalonians 4:16–17: *"For the Lord himself shall descend from Heaven with a shout, with the voice of the archangel, and with the trump of God: and the dead in Christ shall rise first: Then we which are alive and remain shall be caught up together with them in the clouds, to meet the Lord in the air: and so shall we ever be with the Lord."*

After believers are raptured to meet our Lord in the air, we will then stand at the Judgment Seat of Christ. II Corinthians 5:10: *"For we must all appear before the judgment seat of Christ; that every one may receive the things done in his body, according to that he hath done, whether it be good or bad."* Not only will the good be revealed, but also the bad will be revealed at the Judgment Seat of Christ.

While we are standing at the Judgment Seat of Christ, the Tribulation period is taking place on the earth. Paul describes that fearful time period in I Thessalonians 5:2–4. He says, *"For yourselves know perfectly that the day of the Lord so cometh as a thief in the night. For when they shall say, Peace and safety; then sudden destruction cometh upon them, as travail upon a woman with child; and they shall not escape. But ye, brethren, are not in darkness, that that day should overtake you as a thief."* Thank God that the Tribulation is not going to, as a thief in the night, overtake those of us who are believers. We are not children of the night; we are children of the day and will have been taken from this earth before the Tribulation begins.

Are you aware of the analogy that God makes to portray the Tribulation? He compares it to a woman travailing in the pain of childbirth. Perhaps there is no pain known to mankind that is more traumatic than a woman travailing in pain to give birth. Every mother remembers the night the labor pains started. They started out slowly, but as time progressed, so did the intensity of the pain. Even though the labor pains started out slowly, obviously there was more pain after they started than before.

What am I saying? You may think that we are living in terrible times now. The labor pains have not yet begun. Can you imagine a woman being in the pangs of childbirth for seven years with those labor pains never letting up? That is the way that God describes the Tribulation period.

After the seven-year Tribulation period, Jesus is coming back to Earth. We who are saved are coming back to Earth with Him. II Thessalonians 1:7–8: *"And to you who are troubled rest with us, when the Lord Jesus shall be revealed from Heaven with His mighty angels, In flaming fire taking vengeance on them that know not God, and that obey not the gospel of our Lord Jesus Christ:"* This is the conclusion of the War of Armageddon. After the War of Armageddon, the Bible says in Revelation 19:19–20 that the Antichrist and his false prophet are cast into the Lake of Fire.

Then, Jesus sets up His throne on earth. In Revelation 19:16, He is called King of Kings and Lord of Lords. The kingdom of Christ on Earth will last for one thousand years (Revelation 20:6). During that one thousand year reign of Christ, the devil is chained in the bottomless pit (Revelation 20:2). Of the one thousand year reign of Christ, Isaiah 11:9 says, *"...for the earth shall be full of the knowledge of the LORD, as the waters cover the sea."* In those days, there will be no need for Ambassador Baptist College. There will be no need for loudmouthed evangelists. There will be no need for local churches. Everyone will know about the King who reigns on Zion's Hill. Micah 4:3 says that in those days, men will *"beat their swords into plowshares, and their spears into pruning hooks: nation shall not lift up a sword against nation, neither shall they learn war any more."* There will be no need for Annapolis Naval Academy or for West Point. For the first time since the Garden of Eden, man will know "peace on earth, good will toward men."

During the one thousand year reign of Christ, longevity of life will be the norm. Take note sometime of the nine generations listed in Genesis chapter five. Every person lived hundreds of years with the oldest being Methuselah who lived to the ripe old age of 969. The youngest of those listed was Enoch, a mere child of 365. However Enoch went to Heaven without dying. That will be the norm for length of life in the Millennium. Isaiah 65:20 states that if a person dies at the age of one hundred, he will be considered a baby or an infant. In Isaiah 65:22, the days of a man are compared to the days of a tree. Overt rebellion against the King who reigns on Zion's Hill will be the only reason a person will die during the Millennium. Open rebellion will meet with sudden, immediate judgment as Jesus rules with a rod of iron.

From Revelation 20:7, we learn that after the one thousand-year reign of Christ is completed, the devil is loosed for a season. We do not know how long that season is; however, in his last effort, the devil will do his best to deceive the nations. Revelation 20:8 states that his followers will be *"as the sand of the sea."* One may say, "How is that possible? Hasn't Jesus just reigned for one thousand years? Hasn't open rebellion met with sudden, immediate judgment?" I liken it to some young people who have grown up in a Christian home. Though they may conform outwardly, they have not conformed inwardly; and when they get out from under their parents' authority, all of that pent-up rebellion is let loose like a floodtide. That is the way it will be at the end of the millennial reign of Christ. There will be those who have been inwardly rebellious, knowing that if that rebellion were shown overtly, it would meet with sudden, immediate judgment. When the devil is loosed, that pent-up rebellion will be a floodtide (Psalm 66:7). Revelation 20:9 says that God will send fire down from Heaven to devour all those that have followed Satan. Revelation 20:10 then reports that the devil is cast into his ultimate abode—the Lake of Fire.

Now the stage is set for our text passage and the Great White Throne Judgment (Revelation 20:11–15). We will notice four things about this judgment.

The Scene

In Revelation 20, verse 11, John writes, *"And I saw a great white throne, and him that sat on it, from whose face the earth and the Heaven fled away; and there was found no place for them."* Picture this. One day, Heaven is going to roll back as a scroll. God Almighty will burn up this earth and it will cease to be. Heaven is gone. Earth is gone. Unsaved man is standing in outer space staring into the eyes of naked holiness whose eyes are as a flame of fire. Matthew 24:35, Mark 13:31, and Luke 21:33 all state, *"Heaven and earth shall pass away, but my words shall not pass away."* I John 2:17: *"And the world passeth away, and the lust thereof: but he that doeth the will of God abideth for ever."* Heaven cannot stand to stare on the holiness of God. Earth cannot gaze upon His glory. Simply at the face of Jesus Christ, they are compelled to flee away.

Have you considered the Shekhinah glory of God in the Old Testament? Whenever God appeared to man on Earth, it is termed the Shekhinah glory of God. For instance, in Exodus 33:23, Moses went up to the Mount the second time. The Bible says that Moses could not view the face of God because no man can view the face of God and live. Moses could only view the hinder parts of God. When he came down from the mount, the Bible says that his face was as radiant as the noonday sun, so he put a veil over his face. Yet Moses saw only the hinder parts of God. In Exodus 24, the children of Israel were miles away when the glory of God appeared upon the mount. A barrier surrounded the mount beyond which no one could go. Those who penetrated that barrier would be shot through with a dart. Though they were miles away, Exodus 24:17 says, *"And the sight of the glory of the LORD was like devouring fire on the top of the mount in the eyes of the children of Israel."*

In Matthew 17, Peter, James, and John go up to the Mount of Transfiguration with Christ. The word "transfigure" means to "unveil." When the Shekhinah glory of God was unveiled on the mount, the Bible says that the face of Jesus Christ was brighter than the noonday sun. His clothing was whiter than any fuller's soap could make it. Matthew 17:6 says that when the disciples saw the glory of God and heard the voice from Heaven, they *"…fell on their faces, and were sore afraid."* They could not stare upon the Shekhinah glory of God.

Recall Acts 9:6. Saul of Tarsus is on his way to Damascus at midday when he gets a glimpse of the Shekhinah glory of God. For three days and three nights after this encounter, Paul (Saul of Tarsus) was unable to see anything. Later in Paul's writings he mentions that he had a thorn in the flesh. Most Bible scholars believe that he had eye problems. I contend to you that if he had an eye problem, it began that day when he got a glimpse of the Shekhinah glory of God.

Revelation 6 through Revelation 19 lists the judgments of God poured out upon the earth during the Tribulation. At one juncture, the waters will become as blood. A young man will go to the spigot to get a glass of water, but instead he will come back with a glass full of blood-colored water. He will prepare for his daily bath but will only be able to draw a bathtub full of blood-colored water. In those days, the sun will become scorching hot. Men will have grievous sores over their entire bodies and will gnaw their tongues with pain. At another junction of the Tribulation, God will command the bottomless pit to vomit up giant, demon-like locusts. The locusts will have the shape of a horse, a face like a man, the hair of a woman, teeth like a lion, and a tail like a scorpion. Usually locusts live on vegetation, but God is going to command these locusts not to touch any vegetation. Their food will be every man, woman, boy, and girl who has received the mark of the Antichrist and has fallen down to worship him or his image. God will conclude the Tribulation period by causing the Heavens to rain one hundred-pound hail stones.

However, not one time during all these catastrophic judgments do you hear man screaming to flee from the judgments. Do you know what it is that he cannot stand above all else? He cannot stand to stare on the Shekhinah glory of God. Revelation 6:15–16: *"And the kings of the earth, and the great men, and the rich men, and the chief captains, and the mighty men, and every bondman, and every free man, hid themselves in the dens and in the rocks of the mountains; And said to the mountains and rocks, 'Fall on us, and hide us from*—the hail? No. The locusts? No.—*from the face of him that sitteth on the throne, and from the wrath of the Lamb:"*

Years ago, as I was in Troy, Ohio, preaching a revival meeting, the pastor asked if I would go to the TV studio and record some programs. I said, "Preacher, I would be glad to." We drove to Dayton, and I spent quite some time standing under very bright lights videoing some programs for the future. Without thinking I glanced up at those bright floodlights, and when I looked away I saw a myriad of black spots before my eyes. I said, "Pastor, how bright do you think those lights are?" (You perhaps are aware that many years ago I was diagnosed with an eye disease that could possibly cause blindness someday. God has preserved my vision through two corneal transplants and three cataract procedures. But even though my vision has been preserved, my eyes are very sensitive to light.) The pastor responded to my query by saying that he had been told that the lights had one thousand-watt bulbs. Is it any wonder that after only a brief glance at the lights, for a few seconds all I could see was black spots.

The pastor then related an interesting story to me. In India, there was a missionary doctor who ministered primarily to Hindu people in his dispensary. You likely are aware that Hindus worship millions of gods. Among the gods that this particular Hindu worshipped was the sun. He came into the dispensary one day saying, "Doctor, Doctor, I am blind. Can you help me?" The doctor inquired as to how long the man had been blind and how the blindness happened. The man replied, "Sir, I am a Hindu, and among the gods that I worship is the sun. In my worship today, I determined to sit and stare at the noonday sun for two hours. After my worship, I am unable to see anything." The doctor said, "Sir, I am sorry for you. I cannot help you to see physically. No one can stare at a noonday sun for two hours and ever expect to see again. Whereas I cannot help you to see physically, I can help you to see spiritually." He then led the man to a saving knowledge of Christ. What am I saying? You would be an utter fool to sit down at noon and stare at the sun for ten minutes. It could affect your eyes for the rest of your life. How will you ever stand at the judgment bar of God and stare into the face of naked holiness whose countenance is a million times brighter than the noonday sun? Think of it.

The Subjects

Note Revelation 20, verse 12: *"And I saw the dead, small and great, stand before God...."* That is big sinners and little sinners alike. Some say, "Is it not hard to get a person truly saved?" Not most places. It is hard to get a person lost. And a person cannot be saved until he realizes he is lost! Dear unsaved friend who may be reading these words, before the Supreme Court justice of the universe and for the first time in your existence, when you stand at God's Great White Throne Judgment, you will view pure, unadulterated justice. The Bible says in Romans 3:19: *"... that every mouth may be stopped, and all the world may become guilty before God."* Romans 2:1: *"Therefore thou art inexcusable, O man...."* Romans 1:20: *"...so that they are without excuse:"* Jonathan Edwards, in his sermon "Sinners in the Hands of an Angry God," said this, "There is no security in the feeble excuses of unsaved people to keep them out of Hell one second." Some may say, "Well, I believe that you suffer your Hell here on Earth." There is no security in that. Another may say, "I don't believe that a loving God would condemn a soul to Hell." To say that there is no Hell is to say that man is smarter than God. Has not man created penal institutions to separate criminals from society? There is no security in any of your excuses.

The Significance

Revelation 20:12–13: *"And I saw the dead, small and great, stand before God; and the books were opened: and another book was opened, which is the book of life: and the dead were judged out of those things which were written in the books, according to their works. And the sea gave up the dead which were in it; and death and Hell delivered up the dead which were in them: and they were judged every man according to their works."*

Every man is judged according to his works. It is already a foregone conclusion that everyone judged at the Great White Throne will be cast into the Lake of Fire. Why then are they standing there? They stand at that judgment bar to receive their degree of punishment in the Lake of Fire. Psalm 62:12: *"Also unto thee, O Lord, belongeth mercy: for thou renderest to every man according to his work."* Jeremiah 17:10: *"I the LORD search the heart, I try the reins, even to give every man according to his ways, and according to the fruit of his doings."* Romans 2:6: *"Who will render to every man according to his deeds:"* Romans 2:16: *"In the day when God shall judge the secrets of men by Jesus Christ according to my gospel."* Hell will be a million times hotter for a person who attends a Bible-preaching church and dies without Christ than it will be for the person from the liberal church who dies and goes to Hell never having heard the Word of God preached.

The Bible says that the books are opened. What books might that be? I guarantee that the first book to be opened will be **the Bible.** Romans 2:2 says that man will be judged *"according to truth."* The Bible is the truth, the whole truth, and nothing but the truth. In John 12:48, Jesus said, *"He that rejecteth me, and receiveth not my words, hath one that judgeth him: the word that I have spoken, the same shall judge him in the last day."* Every liberal preacher who denies the Bible to be the Word of God will have the same Bible that he denies be his judge when he stands at the Great White Throne.

Many years ago, I was preaching in Jacksonville, North Carolina. On Monday night, a lady who visited in our services approached me after the service and was very complimentary. She said, "Brother Comfort, I really enjoyed the service. I was saved as a little girl and for years my heart has hungered to hear the old-fashioned gospel. I have heard it tonight." I said, "Ma'am, do you know your problem? You are sitting in the wrong pew. You ought to consider changing pews. Every time the doors of this church are open, the same Bible I preached tonight is preached from this pulpit. You ought to consider changing pews." She said, "Tomorrow I am getting on the phone and calling every Baptist preacher in Jacksonville. I am going to take a survey as to how many Baptist preachers in this town still preach the old-fashioned gospel." I said, "I would be interested as to what you find. Please let me know the results of your survey. On Tuesday, she started alphabetically through the phone directory listing of Baptist churches. The man listed first was pastor of the largest Southern Baptist Church in Jacksonville. She called him and said, "Sir, I am taking a survey. I am trying to find out how many Baptist churches in Jacksonville, North Carolina, still preach the old-fashioned gospel. Do you?" He said, "Ma'am, I think that I can save you some time. I do not know of any Baptist church in Jacksonville that still preaches the old-fashioned Gospel except Bible Baptist Church (the church in which I was preaching at the time). I do not think that message is relevant to twentieth-century man." On Friday night, just four days later, this preacher's body was in a casket! If he died the way he lived, when he stands before God, God will merely open to John 3:18 and say, "Condemned! Because you have not believed on the name of the only-begotten Son of God."

The Bible will be at this judgment. But in addition, **the "Book of Man's Sins"** will also be there. Malachi 3:16 terms it a "Book of Remembrance." Matthew 12:36 states, "*...That every idle word that men shall speak, they shall give account thereof in the day of judgment.*" Every time an unsaved person has used God's name in vain, it will add to his torment in the Lake of Fire. I was at a CVS drugstore near my home some time ago. During the length of time it took for me to purchase a very few items, the young lady behind the counter used God's name in vain four times. I said, "Young lady, do you realize that in less than one minute, you have used God's name in vain four times?" I am sickened to hear in our fundamental Baptist churches young people and adults alike who call themselves believers say, "Oh, my God." My dear friend, God's first name is not "my," and He will not hold him guiltless who takes His name in vain.

I once heard of a preacher who was counselor for a group of rowdy boys at a Christian camp. He was quite certain that when he left the cabin, these boys started telling dirty, off-color, double-meaning jokes. He thought he would have a little fun with them while also teaching them a good lesson. Since he had brought his recorder with him to camp, he put it under the bed, pushed the "record" button, turned up the volume so that he could get their conversation, and left the cabin. He stayed for an hour or so before returning to censor the tape. Half of what was on the tape was not fit to be heard. The next morning in chapel he announced, "Fellows and girls, sit back. I have something you are really going to enjoy." He turned on the recorder, and after only a few seconds, one boy recognized his voice and shouted, "That's me! Turn it off." Another boy said, "Oh no! That's me! Break that thing!" They blushed with embarrassment when everyone began to hear in public what they had said in secret. That is a vivid picture of the judgment bar of God where the secret sins (Luke 12:2–3) will one day be made public.

Not only will the Bible and the "Book of Man's Sins" be at the Great White Throne Judgment, but also, **the Book of Life** will be there (Matthew 7:21–23). Some may come to God and say, "God, I was a member of an independent Baptist church." God will say, "The church roll and the Book of Life are not synonymous. Your name is not in the book; I never knew you." My reader friend, if I were not sure my name was in the Book of Life, I would make absolutely certain at this moment.

The Sentence

Notice Revelation 20, verse 15: *"And whosoever was not found written in the book of life was cast into the lake of fire."* How do you feel when you read that verse? I sincerely cannot read that verse without having tears in my heart, if not tears in my eyes.

I hope you do not joke about Hell, but if you do know any jokes about Hell, you had best forget them. There are three things about which I do not joke. I do not joke about God. He is not a joke; He is a holy God. I get nervous when I am in the presence of someone telling a joke about the pearly gates, because sooner or later, God is going to be made a part of that equation. Please leave God out of your jokes. He is not a joke. He is a holy God. Secondly, I do not joke about the Bible. It is a Holy Bible—God's Word. Thirdly, I do not joke about Hell. I was in the presence of a prominent preacher whose name most Christians would recognize, and he told a joke about Hell. I did not laugh. There is nothing that you could say about Hell that could make me laugh. I wish that I could preach like our Seventh-Day Adventist friends that one day Hell is going to burn up and cease to be. Oh! How I wish I could preach that! But Jesus did not say that. Matthew 25:41: *"Then shall he say also unto them on the left hand, Depart from me, ye cursed, into everlasting fire, prepared for the devil and his angels:"* Matthew 25:46: *"And these shall go away into everlasting punishment: but the righteous into life eternal."*

Why will I not laugh about Hell? On Fridays, I pray for my family: cousins, nieces, nephews, in-laws, anybody that is related to me. I pray for my immediate family every day, but on Friday, I pray for even my extended family. If I showed you my original Friday prayer list, you would see my Uncle Walt's name, but it is crossed out. He died without Christ. You would see my Uncle Jim's name, but it, too, is crossed out. He died without Jesus Christ. You would see that my cousin Richie's name, my Aunt Doris' name, and my Aunt Alice's name are also crossed out. They all died without Christ. It is no joke to me that I have more loved ones already suffering in Hell and others that are right now only one heartbeat away from an eternal Hell.

One summer many years ago, as we pulled our trailer across America, we closed a meeting on Sunday and were not to begin another meeting until the next Sunday. I approached my wife and three daughters about using some of our days off to visit my mother whom I had not seen in quite some time. My mother spent thirty to forty years in mental institutions throughout New York and Pennsylvania. Throughout those years, my mother had dozens of shock treatments in her body. Anybody that has ever experienced shock treatments will tell you that nothing more traumatic has ever happened in his or her life. Shock treatments are designed to remake a person emotionally and psychologically. When my brother and I were in college, we visited Mother in the Creedmoor Hospital in Long Island, New York. As we walked down the halls of this mental institution, I heard the weirdest screams and cries that I have ever heard in my life. These screams and cries pierced through my body like an arrow. I could not wait to get out of that place. As we exited the hospital, I recall remarking to my brother, "Bill, if a person is not insane before going into a place like this he will likely be insane before being in it long." My mother died in the Elmira, New York, Psychiatric Center in 1991.

That summer as my family and I went to New York to see Mother, we found her living in a third story apartment in Horseheads, a suburb of Elmira. It was the middle of July and almost 100 degrees ground level. I asked my family to remain in our truck while I checked to see if Mother was at home. I walked up a rickety staircase with a huge German shepherd dog chained to the railing. It seemed like every time the dog barked, the entire staircase shook. I walked up the stairs, knocked on the door and Mother herself answered the door. As I stood in the doorway, I could see all three rooms in her apartment. I was amazed at what I saw. Even though I had only lived with my mother for the first seven years of my life, I remember so vividly how immaculate my mother was concerning her house. My dad would bring in his buddies and my mother would walk behind picking up dirt or lint. She hated dirt. However, as I stood in the doorway of her apartment, I could not believe what I was seeing. Junk, garbage, trash, books, and magazines were piled everywhere. It was a veritable garbage dump. I gave my mother a hug and kiss and told her I loved her. I shook hands with her husband Ken and invited both of them to go with my family to a restaurant so that I could treat them to dinner. Then we would come back to the apartment so that I could talk with them for just a few minutes. They agreed that it was a good plan. When we went to eat, I encouraged them to order anything on the menu that sounded good to them. After dinner, I took them to the grocery store and told Mother to purchase anything she needed, and I would pick up the tab. Upon returning to the apartment, I said, "Can we please sit down now for a little while, as I would like to bare my heart with you?" Ken jumped up and started out the door, but I called him back into the room and reminded him that he had agreed to sit down and talk with me. He reluctantly agreed and sat down. I sat right in front of my mother where I could look into her eyes. I can never remember a time in my life when my heart was as tender as it was that day. I looked into my mother's eyes and rehearsed in my mind: thirty-five to forty years in mental institutions, dozens of shock treatments in her body, and now to have to live in a rat hole like this. I said, "Mother, most people would say that what you have experienced has been a life of Hell on Earth, but Mother, please don't believe it. As hard as it has been, what you have experienced has been a Garden of Eden compared to an eternal Hell. Mother, as difficult as life has been for you, the thing that breaks my heart is that if you are not saved, you will have to spend eternity in Hell. Because God is holy and just, He will one day take you bodily and cast you into the pit, close the pit, and forget about you for ever and ever and ever. Mother, won't you trust Christ as your Savior?" Though my mother made a profession of faith in Christ, she still continued to worship the relics of the Catholic church. Only God knows whether or not I will see my dear mother in Heaven.

One day after the last sinner is banished into Hell, God Almighty will throw back His head and let out with a guffaw that will echo through the corridors of eternity. You may say, "Where do you find that in Scripture?" Proverbs 1:24–26 states, *"Because I have called, and ye refused; I have stretched out my hand, and no man*

regarded; But ye have set at nought all my counsel, and would none
of my reproof: I also will laugh at your calamity; I will mock when
your fear cometh;" Psalm 2:1–4: *"Why do the heathen rage, and the*
people imagine a vain thing? The kings of the earth set themselves, and
the rulers take counsel together, against the LORD, and against his
anointed, saying, Let us break their bands asunder, and cast away their
cords from us. He that sitteth in the Heavens shall laugh: the Lord shall
have them in derision."

Even if you could take the billion-degree flames out of Hell, it
would still be Hell. The worst thing about Hell is to be banished
from God for all eternity, hearing the laughter of a holy God echo
through the corridors of eternity. You may say, "Brother Comfort,
why will God laugh? Will He laugh because people are being
tormented in Hell?" Never believe that! He is not willing that any
should perish. He has no pleasure in the death of the wicked. I
submit to you that there are three reasons that He will laugh. First
of all, God will laugh because sin has been subdued. Secondly,
He will laugh because righteousness has prevailed, and thirdly,
because wickedness is banished forever.

> I dreamed that the great judgment morning
> Had dawned, and the trumpet had blown;
> I dreamed that the nations had gathered
> To judgment before the white throne;
> From the throne came a bright, shining angel,
> And stood on the land and the sea,
> And he swore with his hand raised to Heaven,
> That time was no longer to be.
>
> And, oh, what a weeping and wailing,
> As the lost were told of their fate;
> They cried for the rocks and the mountains,
> They prayed, but their prayer was too late.

—Bertram H. Shadduck

Chapter 10
Practical Aspects
of the Second Coming

Daniel 12:4: *"But thou, O Daniel, shut up the words, and seal the book, even to the time of the end: many shall run to and fro, and knowledge shall be increased."*

If I were to do a study on the book of Daniel, I would divide the book into two sections. The first part of the book of Daniel is the practical section, while the last part is prophetic. Since Daniel chapter twelve in its entirety is prophetic, our text verse would go under the second heading. The chapter begins with a description of a period of time totally unprecedented in the history of the human race. Daniel then continues by delineating the characteristics of that period of time which is commonly called the Tribulation Period.

In Daniel 12:4, Daniel states that the last times will be characterized by two things. First of all, *"Many shall run to and fro."* This phrase indicates an increase in travel. Is it not true that we are living in such a day? In the mid 1960's, I was a member of a church near Greensboro, North Carolina. My pastor at that time said, "Brother Ron, when I was a little boy, I would spend my Sunday afternoons counting the cars as they traveled up and down the highway near my home. It was a tremendously exciting Sunday afternoon when I could count as many as twelve automobiles." That sounds unbelievable in our fast-tracked world. The automobile in most cities has divided the human race between the quick and the dead! No matter where we go, even in impoverished, third-world countries, the highways are lined with automobiles. We are truly living in days of increased travel.

Secondly, Daniel 12:4, states that in the end times, *"knowledge shall be increased."* Someone has said that in the last twenty years, more scientific achievements and more technological advancements have been accomplished than in the previous six thousand years of history. I am not sure whether or not that is true, but I suspect that it may be. It never ceases to amaze me that though I make a reservation on an airline several months before my flight, on the scheduled day of travel, I can go to a computerized kiosk in the airport, enter my name and flight number, and all of the information related to my flight is relayed back to me within a matter of seconds. To me that is mind-boggling. If I had tried to explain that process to a person fifty years ago, I would have been laughed out of town. We are living in a tremendously computerized society.

However, I do not believe it was increased technology that God had in mind in verse four when He said that in the end times, *"knowledge shall be increased."* I believe that God is saying that in the last days, knowledge about the end times would be increased. We are living in that day.

Before 1948, there was very little preaching on the Second Coming of Jesus Christ. If you read books by great men of God from years gone by, such as D.L. Moody, R.A. Torrey, Billy Sunday, and Charles Haddon Spurgeon, you will find very few sermons on the Second Coming of Christ. A man told me that he had a collection of 3,300 sermons that Spurgeon had in print. He had categorized them by topic. Of those 3,300 sermons, only six sermons dealt with the Second Coming of Christ. If I go into a church and preach ten times in one week, I may preach six times on subjects relating to the end times. In a biography of Billy Sunday that our family read, the book stated that he preached once in every revival crusade on the Second Coming. Do you know the problem with that? His evangelistic meetings many times lasted for six to eight weeks. In Billy Sunday's lifetime, he held 350 revival meetings. In my first 25 years in evangelism, I held 800 revival meetings. What is the difference? My meetings last for six days; Billy Sunday's meetings lasted for six weeks or longer, yet he preached only one time on the Second Coming of Christ. If I preached in your town for six weeks, and I preached only one time on the Second Coming of Christ, I do not know what I would say the rest of the time.

What am I saying? Since 1948, when Israel became a sovereign nation, there has been a deluge of preaching on the Second Coming. Every major radio preacher has preached series after series on the Second Coming of Christ. Nearly every Bible-believing pastor has preached many, many, many Sundays on the Second Coming. An elderly Scottish preacher in Staten Island said, "Ron, I preached seventy-five consecutive Sundays on the Second Coming of Christ. Then I followed it with three years going verse by verse through the book of the Revelation."

Have you ever wondered why the avalanche of preaching on the Second Coming is unique to this generation? I believe this is in keeping with a biblical principle. In the Bible, whenever God sends His judgment, He always sends a preacher or a prophet along to announce that the judgment is coming. I believe that today God is sending His prophets around the world to announce that judgment is approaching. I believe that there is only one thing left for every fundamental preacher to preach: "Get right with God. Jesus is coming soon!"

However, Satan inevitably does his best to pervert or counterfeit any good thing. The late nineteenth century was the heyday of real, genuine revivals. However, out of those great revivals, the cults were born. There were many excesses. In this same way, I believe that the devil has had great success in perverting the prophetic message. I know people who will travel all over America to prophetic conferences because they love to have their ears tickled. They can tell you all about the ten toes on Daniel's image. They can even tell you about the toenails on the toes, and yet they have never even tried to win anyone to Christ. I care not how much knowledge you have stored up in your cranium about the Second Coming. If your knowledge does not motivate you to walk in obedience to God, then you have a perverted view of the Second Coming of Christ.

Some have said to me, "Brother Comfort, do you know that I read in a pamphlet recently that in Israel the buzzards are now laying four eggs instead of one? Doesn't that prove that Jesus is coming soon?" I am going to tell you what that proves. Remember the numbers four and one as they are very significant. That statement proves only that they have a lot of healthy buzzards in Jerusalem! Let's be logical. What if the buzzards are laying four eggs today and tomorrow they quit laying four eggs. Does that mean that Jesus is not coming soon? Of course not. I had a preacher tell me, "Brother Comfort, I was in the Bible lands not long ago, and I asked my Jewish guide if the buzzards were really laying four eggs instead of one. He said, 'If that is true, nobody around here has heard anything about it. That is preposterous.'"

Every disciple in Jesus' day was expecting Christ to come in his lifetime. Peter said in I Peter 5:4: *"And when the chief Shepherd shall appear, ye shall receive a crown of glory that fadeth not away."* James said in James 5:8–9: *"Be ye also patient; stablish your hearts: for the coming of the Lord draweth nigh....Behold, the judge standeth before the door."* Paul said in Philippians 3:20: *"For our conversation is in Heaven; from whence also we look for the Saviour, the Lord Jesus Christ:"* John said in I John 2:28: *"And now, little children, abide in him; that, when he shall appear, we may have confidence, and not be ashamed before him at his coming."* What prompted the disciples to look for the Second Coming in their lifetime? They looked for the Lord's return, not because of what they saw in the sky, but because of what they read in the Scriptures. Many Christians today are gazing when they ought to be going.

In this chapter, I am taking a somewhat different approach to the Second Coming of Christ. I draw your attention to the practical aspects of Christ's coming. I do not believe that there is a phase of our lives that will not be affected if we are looking for the Second Coming.

The Second Coming of Christ Should Produce Salvation or Regeneration.

Acts 3:19–20: *"Repent ye therefore, and be converted, that your sins may be blotted out, when the times of refreshing shall come from the presence of the Lord; And he shall send Jesus Christ, which before was preached unto you:"* One day, Peter stood and boldly preached that the sun is going to become black as sackcloth of hair. The moon will turn to blood. The stars are going to fall from their sockets. He preached that in view of the notable day of the Lord, men must repent. No unsaved person who reads these words and believes what the Bible says about the Second Coming of Christ will reject the Savior. Do you realize, my friend, that if Jesus comes today and you are not converted, your eternal destiny is already settled? You will go through seven years of hell on earth, called the Tribulation. Then later, you will stand at the Great White Throne Judgment of God to be cast into a Lake of Fire forever and ever. If Jesus comes right now and you are left behind, it is all over for you. No intelligent unsaved person could believe these truths and reject Christ.

I enumerate three reasons why the knowledge that Jesus is coming soon should produce salvation in the heart of the unbeliever.

It will be **a time of separation**. I Thessalonians 4:16–17: *"For the Lord himself shall descend from Heaven with a shout, with the voice of the archangel, and with the trump of God: and the dead in Christ shall rise first: Then we which are alive and remain shall be caught up together with them in the clouds, to meet the Lord in the air: and so shall we ever be with the Lord."* There is a two-word qualifying phrase in that passage: those who are *"in Christ."* Are you in Christ? The longer I preach, the more I am convinced that a good percentage of the people in our fundamental Baptist church membership have never been born again. I am not talking about the liberal, modernistic churches. I believe that if Jesus Christ came on Sunday morning, you and I would be surprised at the host of people left behind in the church pews.

Are you in Christ? For the first seven years of my life, I was in a Roman Catholic Church, but I was not in Christ. For the next eight years of my life, I was in a Southern Baptist church, but I was not in Christ. I was as lost as a Southern Baptist as I was as a Roman Catholic. During the years I lived in Asheville, North Carolina, as an unsaved boy, I traveled many times with a Southern Baptist preacher, singing in his revival meetings. If Jesus had come during those eight years, I would have been left behind. I was not in Christ. Are you in Christ?

Matthew 24:40–41: *"Then shall two be in the field; the one shall be taken, and the other left. Two women shall be grinding at the mill; the one shall be taken, and the other left."* I am aware that Matthew 24 does not deal with the Rapture, but rather with the Tribulation. Some say that we are living in the days of Matthew 24. I thank God that we are not going to live in the days of Matthew 24. That is the Tribulation period. Matthew 24:40 and 41, in reference to the Tribulation, simply mean that when Jesus Christ comes and the Rapture takes place, there will be one taken in the judgments,

consumed in the judgments of the Tribulation, and the other one
left to endure the judgments of the Tribulation.

Many apply this Scripture to the Rapture. It could very well be
true that a man and his wife may be in bed together when Jesus
comes. Jesus may come in the middle of the night. The wife is
saved; the husband is not. What happens? The wife goes to meet
Christ; her bed clothes are lying unnaturally behind. The next
morning the husband gets up and sees her bed clothes lying on
the bed. He goes to the kitchen, "Honey, are you in there?" She is
not there. He goes to the living room, "Honey, are you there?" She
is not. Why can he not find her? She was in Christ and now she
has been raptured. He is not in Christ; he is left behind. You may
be an unsaved mother with a small baby asleep in the bedroom. If
Jesus comes at this moment, the baby will be taken, and you will
be left behind to endure seven years of hell on earth and later a
Lake of Fire forever and forever.

I remember preaching in Atlanta, Georgia, and a man with whom
I had graduated from Bob Jones University came to me and said,
"Brother Comfort, do you remember me?" I said, "I surely do.
We graduated together in 1961." He said, "Yes, sir. But Ron, do
you know that in the twenty years since I have graduated, I have
never had one moment's assurance that I am born again." Before
that week was over, my college classmate got down on his knees
beside the front pew of the church auditorium and received
Jesus Christ as His Lord and Savior. I left that meeting and went
to Wilmington, North Carolina. A young lady who was reared
in a Christian home, graduated from a Christian high school
and from Tennessee Temple University, and was now teaching
in Wilmington Christian Academy got saved in that meeting.
Margaret said, "Brother Comfort, all of my life I had it up here in
my head. I knew the language; I knew the answers; but I never
had it down here in my heart." Her co-worker, a graduate of Bob

Jones University, teaching in Wilmington Christian Academy, also came down the aisle in that same revival week and trusted Christ as Savior. Friend, are you in Christ? I believe that as Christian parents, we may very well have reared a generation of young people who have second generation Christianity: a theology in their head, but in many cases, not a Christ in their heart.

It will be **a time of deception.** The Bible teaches that one day on this sin-cursed earth, a satanically-energized superman whom the Bible identifies as the Antichrist will cause the whole world to fall down and worship him. Think about this tremendously significant quote: "The mood is well expressed by Henry Spaak, one of the early planners of the Common Market and former Secretary General of NATO. He said, 'We do not want another committee, we have too many already. What we want is a man of sufficient stature to hold the allegiance of all of the people and to lift us up out of the economic morass into which we are sinking.' He said, 'Send us such a man, and be he god or be he devil, we will receive him.'" The world does not care whether it is God or the devil that solves their problems; they just want someone to solve their problems.

If young people will have pictures of Alice Cooper, Mick Jagger, Prince, or other perverted entertainers or even homosexuals on their bedroom walls, do not you think that they will easily fall down before the Antichrist? I was in Tennessee when Elvis Presley died. Every single day, the newspaper headlines read, "Elvis Presley...Elvis Presley...Elvis Presley..." I will never forget the headline that read, "He was a king; he is still a king; and he will always be a king." No matter to what country we travel— no matter the slant of their eyes, the color of their skin, or their native tongue—they still bow down at the shrine of a rock star... Elvis Presley. Do you not see that the world is ready to receive the Antichrist?

Daniel 7:8 calls him *"the Little Horn."* In II Thessalonians 2:3, he is *"the man of sin."* In II Thessalonians 2:11, he is *"the lie."* Revelation 9:11 calls him *"the king of the bottomless pit."* From II Thessalonians 2:9–12 we learn, *"Even him* (Antichrist), *whose coming is after the working of Satan with all power and signs and lying wonders, And with all deceivableness of unrighteousness in them that perish; because they received not the love of the truth, that they might be saved. And for this cause God shall send them strong delusion, that they should believe a lie: That they all might be damned who believed not the truth, but had pleasure in unrighteousness."* These verses confirm the grave warning that if Jesus Christ comes today and you are left behind, you will be deceived by the Antichrist, and you will not be saved in the Tribulation period.

In Scripture, you will find that God always announces that judgment is coming; however when that judgment comes, He never gives a probationary period as a second chance for those who have already been warned before the judgment began. This is an important principle to remember. The Bible says that because you have not received the love of the truth **now** that you might be saved, God will give you over to believe the lie of the Antichrist.

A young man in Virginia said, "Brother Comfort, I am great student of history. I am not a Christian, but I am a great student of history. Everything that you talked about in your sermon, I can see coming to pass: the one-world government, the one-world monetary system, and the one-world dictator. Anybody with any intelligence can see that. I am not saved now; but if Jesus came tonight, I would be saved in the Tribulation period. You can't make me believe that I would fall down and worship the Antichrist." I said, "My dear friend, let me tell you what the Bible teaches. According to your own profession, you are unsaved, so if Jesus comes tonight, number one, you will go into the Tribulation. Number two, you will not be saved because you have already had an opportunity. You will not be given another opportunity for salvation then. Number three, you **will** fall down and you **will** worship the Antichrist. Number four, according to Revelation 14:9–11, you will be cast into the Lake of Fire with the Antichrist forever and ever and ever." It will be a time of deception.

It will be **a time of tribulation.** According to II Thessalonians 2:3, there is a great departure which I believe is the Rapture of the church. After the Rapture, the Antichrist is revealed to the world. According to Daniel 9:26–27, he befriends the Jews and confirms the covenant with the Jews for seven years. The moment that Antichrist confirms the covenant with the Jews the Tribulation officially begins.

The Tribulation is to last for seven years, and the covenant with the Jews is to last for seven years. During the first half of the Tribulation, the judgments that take place on Earth are brought about by man. The Antichrist comes preaching peace (I Thessalonians 5:3). Daniel 8:25 says that by peace shall the Antichrist destroy many. The Jews think that his covenant with them is a covenant of peace, but Isaiah 28:18 calls it a *"covenant with death."* It is an agreement with Hell.

In the middle of the seven-year covenant, the Antichrist breaks his covenant with the Jews; he turns against the Jews for the last three and one-half years of the Tribulation. The judgments that take place on Earth in the last half of the Tribulation are sent down by God out of Heaven. Do you know what happens when the last half begins? The Bible says in Revelation 8:1 that there is *"silence in Heaven about the space of half an hour."* What does that mean? In Revelation 7, the angelic host and the redeemed chorus are singing *"Hallelujah! Glory and honor and blessing to the Lamb that was slain from the foundation of the world."* Suddenly, the singing stops in Heaven and there is a deafening silence. Why? As the covenant is broken and the last half of the Tribulation begins, the angelic hosts look down on Earth's scene, and they cannot believe what their eyes are beholding.

The angels have witnessed every calamity that has ever taken place. In Isaiah 37, one angel in one night slew 185,000 Assyrians. The angelic host witnessed that spectacle. In Tokyo, Japan, in one earthquake, in one day, 480,000 Japanese people were killed. On the island of Okinawa during the Second World War, the blood of 200,000 casualties spilled in the rivers, and the waters actually took on them the color of blood. The angelic host has witnessed every volcanic eruption. They have witnessed every tornado, every typhoon, and every hurricane. Yet they have never seen anything to compare with what their eyes are beholding at this time. As they look down on Earth's scene, they stand in stunned silence and disbelief. The bottomless pit will vomit up giant locusts. These demon-like locusts will have the shape of a horse, the face of a man, hair like a woman, teeth like a lion, and a tail like a scorpion. These locusts will sting men for five months. Usually locusts live on vegetation, but God is going to command these locusts not to touch any vegetation. Instead of vegetation, their food will be every man, woman, boy, and girl who have bowed down to the Antichrist and received his mark. For five months, men are going to gnaw their tongues with pain. Revelation 6:15–17: *"And the kings of the earth, and the great men, and the rich men, and the chief captains, and the mighty men, and every bondman, and every free man, hid themselves in the dens and in the rocks of the mountains; And said to the mountains and rocks, Fall on us, and hide us from the face of him that sitteth on the throne, and from the wrath of the Lamb: For the great day of his wrath is come; and who shall be able to stand?"* Do you know that there is something, humanly speaking, far worse than dying? It is to be in so much torment and agony and pain that you want to die, but you are unable to die to get out of your agony.

No intelligent person can believe these truths about the last days and reject Jesus Christ.

The Second Coming of Christ Should Produce Sanctification or Righteous Living.

An important principle about prophecy in the Word of God is that whenever the Bible makes a prophetic statement, there is generally a practical application that accompanies that prophetic statement. Someone has said, "Every admonition in the Bible has its root cause in the Second Coming." What does that mean? In other words, God gives a command, "Do this!" Why? "Because Jesus is coming again."

Let me illustrate from Scripture this principle showing that a firm belief in the Second Coming of Christ will produce sanctification or righteous living. I John 3:2–3: *"Beloved, now are we the sons of God, and it doth not yet appear what we shall be: but we know that, when he shall appear, we shall be like him; for we shall see him as he is.* (That is the prophetic utterance. Now verse three follows with the practical application.) *And every man that hath this hope in him purifieth himself, even as he is pure."* Do you see that? If you are looking for the Second Coming, no preacher will need to browbeat you into giving up bad habits. When a Christian is looking for the Second Coming, he will clean up his habits so that he will not be ashamed when Jesus comes again.

I Thessalonians 5:23: *"And the very God of peace sanctify you wholly; and I pray God your whole spirit and soul and body be preserved blameless unto the coming of our Lord Jesus Christ."* Why should I keep my spirit, soul, and body pure? Jesus is coming again. Regardless of the summer temperatures, those who are expecting the eminent return of Christ will be modestly dressed. Regardless of what the peer group does or says, the Christian who is looking for Christ's return will seek to walk circumspectly.

I Timothy 6:14: *"That thou keep this commandment without spot, unrebukeable, until the appearing of our Lord Jesus Christ:"* Why should I live in obedience to the Bible? Why after I get saved should I get baptized and join a local church? Why should I be faithful? Why should I tithe? Why should I obey the Lord? Jesus Christ is coming again.

Titus 2:11–13: *"For the grace of God that bringeth salvation hath appeared to all men, Teaching us that, denying ungodliness and worldly lusts, we should live soberly, righteously, and godly, in this present world; Looking for that blessed hope, and the glorious appearing of the great God and our Saviour Jesus Christ;"* A pastor in the state of Colorado sadly related to me, "Ron, do you know that my organist and her husband had a group of young people over to their house and showed them an R-rated movie. This happened three times to the young people in our church." That man and his wife were not looking for the Second Coming of Jesus Christ. You will not have Hollywood's garbage in your home if you are looking for the Second Coming of Christ.

Colossians 3:1–5: *"If ye then be risen with Christ, seek those things which are above, where Christ sitteth on the right hand of God. Set your affection on things above, not on things on the earth. For ye are dead, and your life is hid with Christ in God. When Christ, who is our life, shall appear, then shall ye also appear with him in glory. Mortify therefore your members which are upon the earth;"* Why should I not be in obedience to my body, but in obedience to my spirit? Jesus Christ is coming again. Why should I put to death the desires of my flesh? Jesus Christ is coming again. A man comes home on Wednesday night and says, "Honey, I've got a headache this evening. I've worked hard all day and am really tired, so I am not going to prayer meeting." Believers must be careful to not allow their bodies to dictate their obedience. The spiritual man comes home and says, "Honey, I've got a headache, but I am not letting my body tell me what to do. I am going to go to prayer meeting because it is right...because I am looking for the Second Coming of Christ."

The Bible says that the man who is looking for the Second Coming of Jesus Christ is going to lay up his treasures in Heaven. Where are your treasures? Except for your unsaved loved ones, is there anything that you would grieve to leave behind if Jesus were to come today? If there is, my friend, your treasures are on Earth. What does money mean to you? I totaled a 31-foot Airstream trailer. Perhaps I should rephrase to say that the person I love more dearly than anybody else in life totaled the 31-foot Airstream trailer. When the dust settled, and we assessed the situation, though all my girls were crying, I said, "Girls, don't cry. We have no injuries, and I see no blood. There is not one thing of eternal value that has been damaged. Not one thing."

What does money mean to you? Many Christians hide behind a tithe. Perhaps you ought to be giving far more than a tithe. Look at giving logically. A family of five living on $50,000 a year gives $5,000 a year to God. That is commendable. On the other hand, if a family of two earns $50,000 a year and gives $5,000 a year to God, that is cheap! Anybody knows that it is easier for two to live on $45,000 a year than for five to live on $45,000 a year. God does not see what you put in the offering plate. He sees what you keep back for yourself. It is a tragedy that everywhere I go the work of Christ is limited by money and manpower.

I was preaching in central Ohio in 1981, and a lady approached me after the evening service asking to talk with me. She was in tears, so I said, "Ma'am, if you will please wait here, I will get a lady counselor to talk with you." She said, "No, I want to talk to you." Her husband was standing beside her. She said, "What I am going to tell you is going to break my husband's heart, but I must tell you." I thought, "Oh no, she is going to get her husband mad at me, and he will want to fight!" I said, "Ma'am, wait here and I will get a woman to talk with you." She said, "No. I want to talk to you." She looked at her husband and said, "Now honey, you start the story, and I will finish it." He said, "My wife has operated a Christian bookstore here in central Ohio for years. She has never received one penny of salary. We just charge enough above the cost of the books to keep the lights on and pay the utilities. It has been totally a labor of love for her. One day, I came to my wife and I said, 'Honey, I love you and I appreciate all you have done. Is there anything that I could get for you in a material way that would show you how much I appreciate your sacrificial service for Christ.' She said, 'Darling, I don't have to think about that very long. I would love some day to go to the Bible lands and walk where Jesus walked.' He said, 'All right, I will save my money until you have enough to go to the Bible lands.'" The wife then picked up the story and said, "You know, Brother Comfort, I already have a reservation to go to the Bible lands, and I have a sum of money in the bank saved for the trip. However, I don't need to go to the Bible lands. You need that money much more for your Far East mission trip than I need to go to the Bible lands." My first thought was, "I can't take that money. This is her reward for faithfulness!" As much as I did not want to receive the gift, it seemed as though God said, "Ron, you hypocrite, why don't you practice what you preach? Don't you preach Luke 6:38, 'Give, and it shall be given unto you.' Why not let her prove it?" I said, "Ma'am, I will accept your gift on one condition, and that is that when I return from the Far East, you will let me save my love offerings to have enough to send you to the Bible lands." She said, "Brother Comfort, you misunderstand. This is not a loan, it is a gift. If God is leading me to do it, who are you to tell me that I cannot?" May I say that the next night she handed me a check for the entire amount of their special savings account. Never in my life have I held money in my hands that I felt was more sacred than that night. When we came back from our Far East mission trip, the first person that I wrote was this godly lady. I rejoiced to tell her that in our three and one-half week trip, we had the privilege of seeing 900 adult professions of faith in Jesus Christ, with every person being counseled individually and receiving follow-up material. She wrote a reply to me thanking God for the privilege to give and for the joy of laying up treasures in Heaven. Today, she is with the Lord and rejoicing in the reward of her generosity. She had learned the true value of money. It is only to be a vehicle by which to serve God.

The Second Coming of Christ Should Produce Soul-Winning or a Readiness to Service.

Romans 13:11–12: *"And that, knowing the time, that now it is high time to awake out of sleep: for now is our salvation nearer than when we believed. The night is far spent, the day is at hand: let us therefore cast off the works of darkness, and let us put on the armour of light."* I Thessalonians 5:6: *"Therefore let us not sleep, as do others; but let us watch and be sober."* Luke 19:13: *"And he called his ten servants, and delivered them ten pounds, and said unto them, Occupy till I come."*

When our evangelistic team traveled to the Far East for the first time, one of our stops was in Japan. I sat on the platform one evening in a Japanese Baptist church, and the missionary was addressing his people. Since I could not understand the missionary's words, my mind wandered for a few minutes, and God brought this thought to me. American fundamental churches support 85% of the missions around the world. In the previous centuries, England has sent out the majority of the missionaries. At the close of the 19th century, 98% of the people of London, England, went to church. Today, less than 5% of the people of London, England, go to church. England no longer sends out missionaries. Instead, we send missionaries to England. If God had not raised up America, can you name another country that could disseminate the gospel around the world like America has done?

When Christopher Columbus went to sea, he was not stargazing. His very name "Christopher" means "Christ-bearer." He knew the significance of his name and knew that he had a purpose in life, and it was to proclaim the message of Christ. I believe with all of my heart that Christopher Columbus was born again. If you have never read the book *The Light and the Glory*, I urge you to do so. It is not a book you will find in the public school library. The author asserts that Christopher Columbus went out to sea to find a new land in which to disseminate the gospel of Jesus Christ. The first thing he did when his boat went ashore on American soil was to get down on his knees and dedicate the new land to Jesus Christ. It is my contention that in 1492, God sent Columbus out to sea to discover the United States of America, the nation that could keep the doors of the gospel open in the 21st century.

As I sat on the platform in that Japanese church, I thought, "What happens if we go to sleep in America? Is there another country that can take our place in sending missionaries around the world?" If we go to sleep in America, the gospel around the world is going to be silenced. Nearly every week of my life, I hear of mission fields closing down and missionaries unable to have their visas renewed. I hear of missionaries who must return from the field because of lack of financial support. Are we going to sleep in America?

The first time that we went to the Philippines, we were told that if we were two hours late for a service, the people would simply wait for us to arrive, that time was of no essence to them. I thought that was a lot of public relations jargon to get us to go to the Philippines. It did not take me long to realize that the statement was true. Going through customs at the airport took about two hours. When our team was finally joined with our host missionary, he said "Ron, I had your first preaching appointment scheduled for you across the city about two hours ago. We are late, but don't worry, I am sure the people will be waiting for you." We piled into his jeepney and sped across Manila like a demon. He was driving; I was not. When we got to the church location, believe me, I was prayed up. There was nothing between my soul and my Savior! We went upstairs to a very young church, only a few months old. The small building was jammed with people. All chairs were filled, and folks were standing at the back. The building was not air-conditioned, and because of the two-hour wait, everyone's clothing was saturated with perspiration. However, I preached to a totally attentive congregation. When I gave the invitation, the aisles were jammed with people coming to get saved.

Following that service, the missionary said to me, "Brother Comfort, your next preaching appointment is back across the city on the airport side. We were to be there about two hours ago, but don't worry, the folks will still be waiting for you." I did wonder about his reasoning ability by not planning a bit better to save some travel time, but perhaps he was endeavoring to find out if I was truly at peace with God by riding with him back and forth across the city. When we arrived at the location of our second service, I met Terry Spears from Richmond, Indiana. Terry and his family had been in Manila about six months and knew very little Tagalog. The congregation met in a car port, and every chair was filled. Though they had been waiting two solid hours, I again preached to a totally attentive congregation, and once again many trusted Christ as Savior.

The national missionary then said to me, "Ron, tomorrow you are going to meet a very interesting man by the name of Dan Cruz. Let me tell you about him. Dan Cruz is a millionaire owning many islands in our country. One night, he was in despair planning to take his own life. Out of boredom, he turned on the radio, and as he was thumbing through the stations, he heard me preach. He said that he listened to me preach four nights in a row. After the fourth night, he phoned me, asking me to come to his island. He said, 'I am ready to commit suicide. Would you come and talk to me?' I said, 'Mr. Cruz, I have heard about you, and I would love to talk with you. However, I am swamped with work. Could one of my workers come and talk to you?' Dan said, 'If anyone comes but you, I am committing suicide.'" The missionary made an appointment with Dan Cruz the next day and led him to Christ. In one week's time, Dan Cruz led over one hundred of his laborers to Jesus Christ. One of Dan's burdens became reaching many of the small islands that have never heard the gospel.

There are 7,000 islands in the Philippines today. Hundreds of inhabited islands have never heard the gospel story. Dan Cruz scheduled a service for us on an island called Sabatan. Before the military regime, Sabatan was called "no man's land" and was closed to communication. After the military regime, the island enjoyed freedom of travel and communication but was still very primitive. To travel to the island, our team sat in the floor of a longboat. During the boat ride, Mr. Cruz gave us some helpful, yet somewhat disturbing information about the island's people. He said, "Ron, I don't know what to expect. These folks have never heard a gospel sermon. They have never seen a white woman. Now Mrs. Brubaker, Mrs. Comfort, don't close your eyes during prayer. I truly don't know what to expect. The men of the island spend most of the day drinking alcohol and live in immorality and incest. Mrs. Comfort, whatever you do, do not let your daughters get more than an arm's length from you." My girls were young at that time, and thus, we were somewhat apprehensive about this situation. When we arrived on the island and left the dock, we started collecting people as we moved toward the one main road in the little town. The island had no electricity, but one man had a generator and had a single light bulb hanging from a wire in the street in front of his house. Once the crowd gathered, the missionary estimated that of the 800 people living on the island, at least 700 of them were crowded around us waiting to see what was in store. The island children flocked around my daughters wanting to touch their skin and their hair. They had never seen a little white girl before, and my youngest happened to have somewhat blonde hair to boot! It was so hot and humid that I had to push the children back just a bit in order to breathe.

As I stood there anticipating preaching that night, I said, "Dear God, if you don't send a holy hush over this crowd of children, our money and our time and our efforts are totally wasted. I can never turn the hearts of these folks to God." As I thought about preaching, I was scared to death, but God directed me to preach a simple message on John 3:16 through an "interrupter." I looked around me. The street was packed with people. The rooftops were filled with people. Men and women were hanging out of the windows and every available space had a body in it. Everywhere I looked I saw a sea of bronze-skinned faces. Yet not one time as I was preaching did I have to say, "Young man, would you please look at me and listen." The little children stood there like they were little wooden soldiers watching every move and listening to every word. I have never sensed the power of God as strongly as I sensed it that night.

When I gave the invitation, scores of people came to be saved. They came from the rooftops. They came from the windows. They pushed through the crowds all around us. After a time, someone approached me to say, "Brother Comfort, the man who owns the house behind us was saved tonight and would like to speak with you. He is seventy-eight years of age, and he just wants to meet you and thank you for coming." They also said, "Another eighty-three year old man over here was saved tonight, and he also wants to thank you for coming." I went to those two old gentlemen, and they grabbed my hand first of all. Then they grabbed me around the neck and began to weep on my shoulder. Let me just say that no love offering that I have ever received in my entire life meant a fraction of what that did to me that night. They said, "Mr. Comfort, we are old men. We do not have much time, but thank God we have peace in our hearts now. Mr. Comfort, this is the very, very first time that we have ever heard that Jesus died on the cross for our sins."

I thought that in a short time the crowd would disperse and the people would return to their homes, but it did not happen. They just stood there as if they were expecting or longing for more. Finally, since darkness had completely overtaken us and the hour was getting late, we began to make our way back to our boat. I assumed that surely the crowd would disperse. They did not. They followed us *en masse*. As we were moving toward the boat dock, they began to shout something. I asked the missionary, "What are they shouting?" He said, "Brother Comfort, they are shouting, 'Come back! Come back! Come back!'" After stumbling along in the darkness, we reached our boat, and began to push out into the river. By this time, tears were streaming down my face. Although it was dark, everyone that I could see in the boat was crying. I could hear sniffles all around me. I said, "Dear God, thank you for calling me to be an ambassador for Jesus Christ. Thank you, dear God, for allowing me to be a part of your plan to reach these people with the Gospel." I looked back on the boat docks, and by the light of the torches, I saw that the young folks had climbed onto the boathouses; they had filled the dock; and as we were rowing down the river they were screaming, "Come back! Come back! Come back!" I have seen that scene in my dreams at night. I have often seen a sea of bronze-skinned faces screaming, "Come back!" But nobody wants to go and tell them.

In 1983, as I was preparing to leave my home in Tennessee to preach the fall semester revival meeting at Maranatha Baptist College, I got a letter from the Filipino missionary. He said, "Ron, I felt you should know that we have had a tremendous typhoon here in the Philippines. You will remember the island of Sabatan where you preached? That island was almost totally destroyed by the typhoon. Hundreds of people were swept from their houses and killed." In the photos that he sent, I could see cold, dead, stiff corpses lying on the beaches of Sabatan. I looked at those snapshots and could not help but to weep. I said, "Oh, thank God that Sabatan had the opportunity to hear the Word of God at least once before this typhoon."

The soon return of our Lord should cause us to examine our priorities and evaluate that which is truly important in the light of eternity. Jesus is coming again, and His imminent return should change our lives!

Chapter 11
Heaven, the Perfect Place

Revelation 21:5: *"And he that sat upon the throne said, Behold, I make all things new. And he said unto me, Write: for these words are true and faithful."*

Someone has said that the three most beautiful words in the English language are the words mother, home, and heaven. The word "heaven" in the Bible may refer to one of three major realms:

- The atmospheric heavens, which are immediately above us and in which we live and move.

- The stellar heavens, which ultimately must include the entire universe.

- The Heaven of heavens, the abode of God.

Some will suggest that my topic in this chapter is not really Heaven, but it is the eternal state. If Heaven means the abode of God, then I can rightly say that what I am discussing is Heaven.

Contrary to what most people think, preparing a sermon on Heaven is perhaps the most difficult of all subjects in the Bible. The enormous difficulty in describing Heaven is illustrated in utterances of the men of God who penned the Bible. For example, Paul says in II Corinthians 12:1–4: *"It is not expedient for me doubtless to glory. I will come to visions and revelations of the Lord. I knew a man in Christ above fourteen years ago, (whether in the body, I cannot tell; or whether out of the body, I cannot tell: God knoweth;) such an one caught up to the third Heaven. And I knew such a man, (whether in the body, or out of the body, I cannot tell: God knoweth;) How that he was caught up into paradise, and heard unspeakable words, which it is not lawful for a man to utter."* Again Paul said in I Corinthians 2:9: *"But as it is written, Eye hath not seen, nor ear heard, neither have entered into the heart of man, the things which God hath prepared for them that love him."* He continues in verse ten and says that God has revealed these things unto us by His spirit. However, we cannot imagine what Heaven is really like because we have never seen nor experienced anything that would come close to the glory of Heaven. God gives us just a little taste of Heaven in our soul so that we can experience the abundant life as we are on our way to Heaven.

In our text, God tells John, *"I make all things new."* Again in Isaiah 65:17, the Lord says, *"For, behold, I create new Heavens and a new earth: and the former shall not be remembered, nor come into mind."*

In Genesis chapter three, we have the story of paradise lost. In Revelation chapters 21 and 22, we have paradise regained. These two chapters tell us about many new things. There will be a new Heaven, a new Earth, a new people, a new temple, a new light, and a new city. In this message, I draw your attention to the New City.

Heaven Is Perfect Purity.

The streets of the city are paved with pure gold. None of this common 14-carat stuff! The gold we know today is imperfect, stained, and clouded, but the gold with which the streets in Heaven are made is transparent and pure.

The Bible states that in Heaven there will be **no curse.** Revelation 22:3: *"And there shall be no more curse: but the throne of God and of the Lamb shall be in it; and his servants shall serve him:"* Genesis 3:17 reads, *"...cursed is the ground for thy sake; in sorrow shalt thou eat of it all the days of thy life."* We are living in a beautiful world, but the scars of the curse are written on everything in nature. You cannot see a beautiful rose without noticing the thorns. No mother can ever hold a little baby in her arms until first she has travailed in birth pains. For every joy, there is sorrow. For every ray of sunshine, there is a dark cloud of gloom. The curse is written everywhere. Job said in Job 5:7: *"Yet man is born unto trouble, as the sparks fly upward."*

In that city there will be no curse, and there will be **no defilement.** Notice Revelation 1:27: *"And there shall in no wise enter into it any thing that defileth, neither whatsoever worketh abomination, or maketh a lie: but they which are written in the Lamb's book of life."* In I Peter 1:3–4, the Bible says, *"Blessed be the God and Father of our Lord Jesus Christ, which according to his abundant mercy hath begotten us again unto a lively hope by the resurrection of Jesus Christ from the dead, To an inheritance incorruptible, and undefiled, and that fadeth not away, reserved in Heaven for you."* In Revelation 22:15, the Word of God says, *"For without are dogs, and sorcerers, and whoremongers, and murderers, and idolaters, and whosoever loveth and maketh a lie."*

The Bible says there shall be **no more darkness.** Revelation 21:23 says, *"And the city had no need of the sun, neither of the moon, to shine in it: for the glory of God did lighten it, and the Lamb is the light thereof."* In verse twenty-five of that same chapter, we read, *"And the gates of it shall not be shut at all by day: for there shall be no night there."* Again God said in Revelation 22:5: *"And there shall be no night there; and they need no candle, neither light of the sun; for the Lord God giveth them light: and they shall reign for ever and ever."*

There will be no need of any creative lighting because Jesus is uncreated light. John 8:12: *"Then spake Jesus again unto them, saying, I am the light of the world: he that followeth me shall not walk in darkness, but shall have the light of life."*

When Moses came down from the mount, his face shone because he had been with God. When Jesus came down from the Mount of Transfiguration, His face shown like Heaven itself. That resplendent light will brighten every eternal day.

Darkness brings heartache. That little girl who has lost her daddy can handle the loneliness all right during the daytime because there will be things to keep her busy. But when the shadows fall, and she places her head on her pillow, the sobs begin. A sweet widow can make it all right throughout the day because there are friends to come for a visit. However, when night falls, there is that feeling of loneliness. The night seems an age, and sleep seems as though it will never come.

Heaven Has a Perfect Population.

This city is a city of perfect population according to Hebrews 12:22–23: *"But ye are come unto mount Sion, and unto the city of the living God, the Heavenly Jerusalem, and to an innumerable company of angels, To the general assembly and church of the firstborn, which are written in Heaven, and to God the Judge of all, and to the spirits of just men made perfect."*

That Scripture lists several groups that populate Heaven.

- God will be there.
- The angels will also be there.
- The church of the firstborn, which means every believer from Adam until the last martyr that is slain in the Tribulation, will be there.
- The spirits of just men made perfect, which may be the Old Testament saints, will be present.
- The people who populate Heaven are so different from the crowd that will populate Hell. Evangelist Oliver Greene used

to preach a sermon entitled, "Your Next Door Neighbor in Hell." He said in that sermon that when a person looks for a house, he wants to live in a good neighborhood, a place where it will be peaceful and enjoyable. No person would purchase a piece of property on which to build a home without first investigating the neighborhood. A thinking husband, planning the future for his family, would not purchase a piece of property on the street of forgotten men, in a settlement of bootleggers, nor in the section where gangsters, dopers, sex offenders, and pedophiles live. A thinking husband and father would purchase a piece of property in a respectable and safe community.

Decent, honest, upright ladies and gentlemen check on whether there is a good school or a good church in the neighborhood in which they want to live. However, if you die in sin and go to Hell, you can expect your next door neighbors to be those who are enumerated in Revelation 21:8: *"But the fearful, and unbelieving, and the abominable, and murderers, and whoremongers, and sorcerers, and idolaters, and all liars, shall have their part in the lake which burneth with fire and brimstone: which is the second death."*

However, Heaven will be populated with **the Heavenly crowd.** In Revelation 21:12, the Bible says, *"... and had twelve gates, and at the gates twelve angels, and names written thereon, which are the names of the twelve tribes of the children of Israel:"* In verse fourteen of the same chapter, we read, *"And the wall of the city had twelve foundations, and in them the names of the twelve apostles of the Lamb."*

The Bible states that the twelve foundations of the city will have the names of the twelve apostles and the twelve tribes of Israel. I take that to mean that the saints of the Old Testament and the New Testament church of Jesus Christ will be there.

- There will be David who once wept for Absalom, but in Heaven, he will be radiant from the glory of God.

- In Heaven, Paul will be exultant where once he sat with his feet in stocks.

- John the Baptist will rejoice, although he had his head cut off in a dark, dreary dungeon.

- Martyrs, whose blood had once reddened the mouths of lions, will sit in the presence of Jesus.

- Savonarola will wear a crown, although he was burned at the stake.

- David Livingston, who died on his knees at his bedside, will perhaps be kneeling before the throne of God.

- John Knox, who rebuked Mary Queen of Scots, Bloody Mary, will be singing with others to the glory of God.

- David Brainerd, who burned out for God at the age of twenty-nine endeavoring to reach the American Indians for Christ, will shine as a star. Daniel 12:3: *"And they that be wise shall shine as the brightness of the firmament; and they that turn many to righteousness as the stars for ever and ever."*

- We will know all these saints who have gone before! Matthew 8:11 says, *"And I say unto you, That many shall come from the east and west, and shall sit down with Abraham, and Isaac, and Jacob, in the kingdom of Heaven."*

We will recognize **our loved ones.** Many times in the Old Testament when a patriarch died, the Bible says he was *"gathered to his people."* That simply means that the patriarch went to be with his family who had preceded him to Heaven. Of course, the connotation is that he knew them on the other side. There is not one doubt in my mind but that we will know our loved ones in that eternal state. Do you not think that we will know more in

Heaven than we do now? If we know our loved ones now, we will certainly know them in Heaven!

Heaven Is Perfect in Power, Peace, and Provision.

This celestial city will be a place of **perfect power** with no corrupt politics. Revelation 22:3: *"And there shall be no more curse: but the throne of God and of the Lamb shall be in it; and his servants shall serve him:"* Revelation 21:24 says, *"And the nations of them which are saved shall walk in the light of it: and the kings of the earth do bring their glory and honour into it."* Verse twenty-six in that same chapter reads, *"And they shall bring the glory and honour of the nations into it."*

Heaven will enjoy **perfect peace.** Revelation 14:13 reads, *"And I heard a voice from Heaven saying unto me, Write, Blessed are the dead which die in the Lord from henceforth: Yea, saith the Spirit, that they may rest from their labours; and their works do follow them."* Revelation 21:4 says, *"And God shall wipe away all tears from their eyes; and there shall be no more death, neither sorrow, nor crying, neither shall there be any more pain: for the former things are passed away."*

The Bible has much to say about weeping.

- Weeping saints: John 16.
- Weeping sinners: Matthew 22.
- Weeping soul-winners: Psalm 126:5–6.
- Weeping sorrowers: John 20.
- Weeping servants: Acts 20:19.
- Weeping Savior: John 11:35.

Since in Heaven there is perfect peace, God will wipe away all tears from our eyes. Whenever man wipes away tears, the tears are bound to come back to our eyes again. But when God wipes them away, He will permanently wipe them away forever.

Today, there are all kinds of tears: tears of bereavement, tears of sympathy and mercy, tears of disappointment, tears over crime and violence, tears of anger and resentment, and tears of pain. There are many hearts that bleed in secret. When we walk those streets of gold, suddenly we will realize that we are looking through eyes that cannot possibly shed tears. Psalm 30:5 says, *"For his anger endureth but a moment; in his favour is life: weeping may endure for a night, but joy cometh in the morning."*

Heaven is a place with **no sickness.** Before the fall of man in the Garden of Eden, Adam never had a headache, toothache, or any bodily ailments. Philippians 3:21 says, *"Who shall change our vile body, that it may be fashioned like unto his glorious body, according to the working whereby he is able even to subdue all things unto himself."* I John 3:2 says, *"Beloved, now are we the sons of God, and it doth not yet appear what we shall be: but we know that, when he shall appear, we shall be like him; for we shall see him as he is."* I Corinthians 15:49 reads, *"And as we have borne the image of the earthy, we shall also bear the image of the Heavenly."* I Corinthians 15:42–44: *"So also is the resurrection of the dead. It is sown in corruption; it is raised in incorruption: It is sown in dishonour; it is raised in glory: it is sown in weakness; it is raised in power: It is sown a natural body; it is raised a spiritual body. There is a natural body, and there is a spiritual body."*

When the Bible says that we shall be like Jesus, it does not mean that we will be like Him spiritually, but rather we will be like Him physically. After Jesus arose from the dead, gravity had no pull on His body. Time had no bearing on His being. He could go through closed doors. He could be here in a moment, and there in a moment. That is the same kind of body that we will possess upon our resurrection: a body incapable of experiencing any type of pain.

The Bible says that in Heaven, there will be no sea. To the ancient, the sea was a fearsome, frightful, awesome monster. Ships in ancient days had no compasses, and when cloudy, stormy days would come, many ships were lost. To the Apostle John exiled on the Isle of Patmos, the sea represented a place where there was much loss of life. Here, he was separated from loved ones by the sea that divided them. He was looking forward to the time when there would be no more fear of death.

Heaven is a place of **no separation.** Heaven is a place where there will be no graves dug and no hearse rolling its dark way to the tomb. Notice this wonderful passage of Scripture. I Corinthians 15:54–57: *"So when this corruptible shall have put on incorruption, and this mortal shall have put on immortality, then shall be brought to pass the saying that is written, Death is swallowed up in victory. O death, where is thy sting? O grave, where is thy victory? The sting of death is sin; and the strength of sin is the law. But thanks be to God, which giveth us the victory through our Lord Jesus Christ."* The Bible also states in I Corinthians 15:26: *"The last enemy that shall be destroyed is death."*

Hallelujah! How I look forward to Heaven!

Heaven is a place of **perfect provision.** Revelation 21:6: *"And he said unto me, It is done. I am Alpha and Omega, the beginning and the end. I will give unto him that is athirst of the fountain of the water of life freely."*

Jesus told the Samaritan woman at the well that the water that He would give her would be a well of water springing up in her unto eternal life. Christ is all I need. He is sufficient for my provisions. Notice Revelation 22:1: *"And he shewed me a pure river of water of life, clear as crystal, proceeding out of the throne of God and of the Lamb."* Our provisions emanate from the throne of God and the Lord Jesus Christ.

Down through the ages, many great cities have been built on rivers. Four rivers branched from the Garden of Eden. London,

Rome, Paris, New York, and Chicago are all built on rivers, but these rivers are contaminated. Earthly streams have their source in some mountain, but the crystal clear stream in Heaven will have its source from the throne of God. Psalm 46:4–5: *"There is a river, the streams whereof shall make glad the city of God, the holy place of the tabernacles of the most High. God is in the midst of her; she shall not be moved: God shall help her, and that right early."*

Revelation 22:2 says, *"In the midst of the street of it, and on either side of the river, was there the tree of life, which bare twelve manner of fruits, and yielded her fruit every month: and the leaves of the tree were for the healing of the nations."* Some would say this is a millennial promise because it speaks of the healing of the nations. This could also be translated as the health or the welfare of the nations. Certainly there will be no sickness, but perfect health in this beautiful city.

Why are there fruit-bearing trees on both sides of the river? Some ask, "Will we eat in Heaven?" When God put Adam in the Garden of Eden, He told him that he could eat of any tree in the garden except the Tree of the Knowledge of Good and Evil. He did not have to eat, but the food was there for him to eat if he so desired. After Jesus arose from the grave, He ate broiled fish with His disciples. He did not have to eat, but He chose to do so. Consider two thoughts here—enjoyment and fellowship.

First of all, the food will be there for **enjoyment.** Everyone that I know enjoys eating, especially fresh fruit. The fruit will add to the enjoyment of Heaven for us. Some of the sweetest fruit that I have ever eaten in my life I enjoyed in the Bible lands. We had oranges, pears, apples, watermelon, figs, and many other types of fruit. I can still get hungry just thinking about that delicious fruit. But my friend, that fruit was all grown still under the curse of sin. I wonder just how the fruit in Heaven will taste.

The second thought I have about food in Heaven pertains to **fellowship.** Most of the time whenever we have fellowship with other believers, we also enjoy food. When you invite friends over after church on Sunday evening, it would be mighty disappointing if there were nothing to eat. I do not think that I have ever been invited to someone's home but what we have had something to eat before the fellowship concluded. I am confident that we will enjoy food around the banquet table of God, as well as fellowship with those who have gone on before. The trees in Heaven will bear twelve manner of fruit—one for every month of the year—and it will be a constant reminder that God is the source of all our provision.

Heaven Is Perfect in Proportions.

As we approach the city, we will first notice **the walls** of jasper, 250 feet high. Walls are typically for protection, but I believe that the walls of the Heavenly city will be for beauty. Jasper is a diamond-colored stone. Imagine a city surrounded by diamond walls 250 feet high! I once saw the crown jewels in London Tower, and in the collection was supposedly the most perfect diamond in the world. This was a diamond of over 1,000 carats. Let me say that in the new city, that diamond will merely be considered dust.

There will be **twelve gates,** each gate of one pearl. I ask you, could the gates be of anything other than pearl? A pearl is the product of suffering. An oyster is a living pump, and when a grain of sand gets inside the oyster, the continuous pumping rubs a sore on the side of the oyster. The oyster then secretes a substance over that grain of sand until one day, that which started as a grain of sand becomes a precious gem. That pearl is the object of a wounded side. As we look on the gates of pearl, we will be reminded that we are in Heaven because of a wounded side.

The Bible teaches us that the city will be foursquare—a perfect size. It will reach 1,500 miles in every direction. A city that size would cover all of Ireland, Britain, France, Spain, Italy, Germany, Austria, Prussia, most of Turkey, and half of Russia. Someone has calculated that if fifteen feet were allowed for each story in that city, there would be 528,000 stories. Each story would contain two and a quarter million square miles. The city would be able to inhabit over 100 billion people. We are told that Earth's population in the 6,000 years has totaled no more than 60 billion. If there were 100 billion people in the New Jerusalem, there would be a bit over thirty-nine square miles for each man, woman, and child. Each story of the city would be 15,000 times the size of London!

The description of **the foundation** of this city leads us to notice its variety of glorious colors. God must be a lover of beauty. The stones on the foundation are emerald, red, crystal, purple, orange, and every beautiful color imaginable.

Have you ever seen a beautiful rainbow glowing in the sky after a spring shower? Though there is no earthly use for the rainbow, we enjoy looking upon it. God took the azure blue of His sky, the beautiful whitecaps of the a raging sea, the emerald green of the verdant meadows, the blazing glory of autumn, the fire of an August sunset, and crystallized them all in the living color of His holy city. What beauty! What splendor!

Dr. Biederwolf tells of a little girl who was blind from birth and only knew the beauties of Earth from her mother's lips. One day, a noted surgeon operated on her eyes, and at last, his operations were successful. As the last bandage fell off, the little girl flew into her mother's arms, then ran to the window and the open door. As all the glorious beauty of the earth rolled across her vision for the first time, she ran back to her mother crying, "Oh, Mama, why didn't you tell me that everything was so beautiful?" As the mother wiped the tears of joy from her little girl's eyes, she said,

"My precious child, I tried to tell you, but I couldn't do it. There were not enough words to explain the beauty of God's creation."

One day, when we go sweeping through those gates of pearl and catch our first vision of the enrapturing beauty all around us, I think we will hunt up the Apostle John and say, "John, why did you not tell us that everything was so beautiful?" He is going to say, "I tried to describe it in Revelation chapters twenty-one and twenty-two, but there were not words in human vocabulary to explain the beauty of God's Heaven."

I have had the privilege of preaching in many foreign countries and forty-seven of our fifty states. I have seen sights that could only make an atheist scratch his head. But my friend, God did all this in six days! Two thousand years ago, Jesus said, "I am going to Heaven to prepare a place for you." For all these years, He has been doing interior decorating. Hallelujah! Heaven must be beautiful!

Heaven Is Perfect Pleasure.

Revelation 11:15 says, *"And the seventh angel sounded; and there were great voices in Heaven, saying, The kingdoms of this world are become the kingdoms of our Lord, and of his Christ; and he shall reign for ever and ever."* Then in Revelation 22:5, we read, *"And there shall be no night there; and they need no candle, neither light of the sun; for the Lord God giveth them light: and they shall reign for ever and ever."*

God shall reign forever and ever, and we will reign with Him. That will be our perfect pleasure.

Revelation 22:3 says, *"And there shall be no more curse: but the throne of God and of the Lamb shall be in it; and his servants shall serve him:"*

Several years ago, I remember hearing two Hollywood actors discussing Heaven on the radio. Like so many people, their conception of Heaven was that they would just sit on a cloud, playing a harp forever and ever. Their conclusion was that that would not be too much enjoyment for them. I, personally, do not think much of their concept of Heaven.

God put Adam and Eve in the Garden of Eden and asked Adam to tend the garden. Adam did not just sit around all day long. He was busy doing things that were enjoyable, serving the One whom he loved. I do not believe that God has created the vastness of the universe for waste or without purpose. Perhaps one day God will come to me and say, "Ron, I am dispatching you to a distant point. I have some business for you to do for me there." Faster than the speed of light, I will be there doing service for my God.

Do you remember what the Queen of Sheba said about Solomon after beholding his kingdom? I Kings 10:7: *"Howbeit I believed not the words, until I came, and mine eyes had seen it: and, behold, the half was not told me: thy wisdom and prosperity exceedeth the fame which I heard."* I Kings 10:8 goes on to say, *"Happy are thy men, happy are these thy servants, which stand continually before thee, and that hear thy wisdom."*

Oh, how glorious it will be to serve Him of Whom Solomon was a type and picture.

Revelation 21:11 says, *"Having the glory of God: and her light was like unto a stone most precious, even like a jasper stone, clear as crystal;"* Revelation 22:4: *"And they shall see his face; and his name shall be in their foreheads."* David said in Psalm 17:15: *"As for me, I will behold thy face in righteousness: I shall be satisfied, when I awake, with thy likeness."* Matthew 5:8 states: *"Blessed are the pure in heart: for they shall see God."*

Jesus said in John 1:18: *"No man hath seen God at any time; the only begotten Son, which is in the bosom of the Father, he hath declared him."*

Moses, when he was on the mountain alone with God, did not see the face of God, but could only see the hinder parts. But we shall see Him! I Peter 1:8 says, *"Whom having not seen, ye love; in whom, though now ye see him not, yet believing, ye rejoice with joy unspeakable and full of glory:"* What joy when faith will be turned into sight!

We will not only see our Lord and serve Him, but we will worship Him. Revelation 1:9 reads, *"And after these things I heard a great voice of much people in Heaven, saying, Alleluia; Salvation, and glory, and honour, and power, unto the Lord our God:"* Revelation 21:22: *"And I saw no temple therein: for the Lord God Almighty and the Lamb are the temple of it."*

When we want to worship, we will not go to a temple, to a church, or to a synagogue. We will worship on the bosom of God. God revealed Himself as God Almighty the first time in Genesis chapter seventeen. In the Hebrew, the word is *El Shaddai*. It has to do with sufficiency—all sufficiency pictured as the many-breasted God. It paints for us the picture of a little baby in the arms of her mother and being nourished and fed at the mother's breast. For that baby, all is right with the world. My friend, all will be right as we worship on the bosom of our Heavenly Father. No signs, symbols, sacraments, systems, or temples will be needed. God and the Lamb are all we need!

However, the supreme pleasure of Heaven will be that we will forever be with Christ. In Revelation 21:3 we read, *"And I heard a great voice out of Heaven saying, Behold, the tabernacle of God is with men, and he will dwell with them, and they shall be his people, and God himself shall be with them, and be their God."*

D. L. Moody had the following words written in the flyleaf of his Bible:

"The light of Heaven is the face of Jesus.
The joy of Heaven is the presence of Jesus.

The melody of Heaven is the name of Jesus.
The harmony of Heaven is the praise of Jesus.
The theme of Heaven is the work of Jesus.
The employment of Heaven is the service of Jesus.
The duration of Heaven is the eternity of Jesus.
The fullness of Heaven is Jesus Himself."

Heaven is to be with Jesus Himself.

Incidentally, there will be gates of pearl; incidentally, there will be streets of gold; incidentally, there will be walls of jasper. But the most wonderful fact about Heaven is that Jesus is there.

It seems as though I can hear the Lord Jesus say, "On what street would you like to live in Glory and which mansion would you like to call home?" I will say, "Dear Lord, any street, any mansion, just so that the window is open toward the palace of the Great King so that I may see Him come and go."

Charles Spurgeon tells the story of one who dreamed a dream of Heaven when in the distress of his mind. He thought he stood in the outer court of Heaven, and he saw the glorious host marching up, singing sweet hymns, bearing the banners of victory; and they passed by him through the gate. When they vanished from sight, he heard in the distance sweet strains of music.

"Who are they?" he asked.

"They are the goodly fellowship of the prophets who have gone on to be with God."

He heaved a deep sigh as he said, "Alas! I am not one of them, and never shall be, and I cannot enter there."

By and by there came another band, equally lovely in appearance and equally triumphant and robed in white. They passed within the portals, and again shouts of welcome were heard within.

"Who are they?"

"They are the goodly fellowship of apostles."

"Alas!" he cried, "I belong not to that fellowship either and I cannot enter there."

He still waited and lingered and hoped that he might yet go in, but the next multitude did not encourage him for they were the noble army of martyrs. He could not go in with them nor wave their palm branches. He waited still.

He saw that the next was a company of preachers and officers of the Christian churches, but he could not go in with them.

At last, as he walked he saw a larger host than all the rest put together, marching and singing most melodiously. In front, walked the woman that was a sinner and the thief that died upon the cross close by the Savior; and he looked long and saw such as Mary Magdalene and the like. When they entered, he could see who they were, and thought, "There will be no shouting about them." But to his astonishment, it seemed as if all Heaven was rent with the seven full shouts as they passed in. And the angel said to him, "These are they that were mighty sinners saved by the grace of God." And he said, "Blessed be God! I can go in with them!"

Blessed be God! You and I, too, can go in with the blood-washed company of sinners. I cannot go in anywhere but with that company.

> "This is my story, this is my song.
> Praising my Savior all the day long."

My friend, after reading this sermon on Heaven, has God spoken to your heart? The only way that you will ever be able to enter Heaven is by receiving Jesus Christ into your heart as your Lord and Savior. Romans 10:9–13 says, *"That if thou shalt confess with thy mouth the Lord Jesus, and shalt believe in thine heart that God hath raised him from the dead, thou shalt be saved. For with the heart man believeth unto righteousness; and with the mouth confession is made unto salvation. For the scripture saith, Whosoever believeth on him shall not be ashamed. For there is no difference between the Jew and the Greek: for the same Lord over all is rich unto all that call upon him. For whosoever shall call upon the name of the Lord shall be saved."*

If you will right now confess to God that you are a sinner, believing in your heart that Jesus Christ died on the cross for your sins and rose again, you can invite Him into your life to save you.

If you want to be saved, simply bow your head and pray this simple prayer.

> *"Dear Lord, I know I am a sinner. I believe that Jesus died on the cross and rose again for my salvation. The best I know how, I am now receiving Him into my heart as my personal Lord and Saviour."*

Do trust the Savior so that you, too, may spend eternity in the beauties of Heaven with our lovely Lord.